MONUMENTAL FRAGMENTS

TRANSMISSION

Transmission denotes the transfer of information, objects or forces from one place to another, from one person to another. Transmission implies urgency, even emergency: a line humming, an alarm sounding, a messenger bearing news. Through Transmission interventions are supported, and opinions overturned. Transmission republishes classic works in philosophy, as it publishes works that re-examine classical philosophical thought. Transmission is the name for what takes place.

MONUMENTAL FRAGMENTS

PLACES OF PHILOSOPHY IN
THE AGE OF DISPERSION

George Vassilacopoulos

re.press

PO Box 40, Prahran, 3181, Melbourne, Australia
http://www.re-press.org

© G. Vassilacopoulos 2013
The moral rights of the authors have been asserted

This work is 'Open Access', published under a creative commons license which
means that you are free to copy, distribute, display, and perform the work as long as you clearly attribute the work to the authors, that you do not use this work for any commercial gain in any form whatsoever and that you in no way alter, transform or build on the work outside of its use in normal academic scholarship without express permission of the author (or their executors) *and* the publisher of this volume. For any reuse or distribution, you must make clear to others the license terms of this work. For more information see the details of the creative commons licence at this website:
http://creativecommons.org/licenses/by-nc-sa/3.0/

National Library of Australia Cataloguing-in-Publication Data

Vassilacopoulos, George, author.

Monumental fragments : places of philosophy in the age of dispersion / George Vassilacopoulos.

9780980305296 (paperback/ebook)

Series: Transmission.
Philosophy.

190

Designed and Typeset by A&R

This book is produced sustainably using plantation timber, and printed in the destination market reducing wastage and excess transport.

CONTENTS

Untitled	9
Rhapsodies of Emptiness	91
Untitled	103
Paradoxes	111
Untitled	113
The Command	131
Untitled	153

For Toula Nicolacopoulos

Fellow thinker and silent witness who teaches that before the clarity of thinking there is the rebellion of loving.

Every word is a doorway
to a gathering, one often cancelled,
and that's when a word is true: when it insists on the gathering.

(Yannis Ritsos, 'The meaning of simplicity',
translation from the Greek)

After Hegel and no longer able to write a manifesto we can only gather the fragments of the gathering of the future.

Philosophy arises in a philosophical world. It is pure conceptuality, the vision that is empty of being, the thinking of being without being, gathered in a single mind as the *topos* of the gathering of visionary concepts. As thinking thought, the thinker expands infinitely to embrace the 'we', albeit only in principle. In this sense his embracing remains unpopulated. The philosopher knows that the house that philosophy builds is to become the dwelling of those who arrive from the distant future. Philosophy is a welcoming from a far. This is the highest manifestation of the gathering's power to 'submit to infinite pain' and withstand its own self as the vortex of otherness. It sinks into the depth of its *kenosis* without losing itself. In and out of this deepening philosophy emerges from the cosmic darkness that the gathering gathers. In philosophy the gathering recollects its being as a *thanatology*—as the dying of its death—through which it practices a defiant and visionary emerging of love out of death—that of the concept and of history.

For the communist poet: we've always lived somewhere else, and only when someone loves us do we return for a little while (Tasos Livaditis). The fragment is the *topos* of this return. If we stay longer we are transformed into philosophers.

To philosophize is to experience the death of those who have yet to be born, ourselves.

The speculative ego, what is it? The place abandoned by the glorious gatherings of the future.

Who are those who come from the future? They are the multitude of the gathered in the gathering. In this multitude the mathematical infinity equals one since every single member expands to embrace the whole gathering by becoming its place of dwelling, its gatherer. Everyone is in everyone. In our era, that of loss and retreat and sorrow, it is the philosopher who performs the gesture of embracing. The philosopher embraces the gathering-we in its retreat as this retreat, stuttering 'we, we…. we'. This is what Hegel keeps repeating from the beginning to the end of the development of his system.

Hegel, the dead philosopher who brought us the future.

The challenge of philosophy today is no longer the 'new'. The challenge is the 'old', or rather the oldest of the old, the place in which philosophy happens as the happening that is philosophy; and it happens in the retreat of the gathering-we. So not the creation of the new but the presencing of what is always present—the presencing of the indeterminate gathering, as the place of redemption of the ones who have already lost everything, even the loss itself.

The philosopher writes on his empty palms.

The speculative syllogism is the vision of the world's pulse.

'Only the dead can enter': sign on the entrance of the inner.

Spinoza, substance; Hegel, world.

To fear the religiosity of the gathering is to fear death.

Between death that is a despairing about love and death that is the vision of love there is the fragment. Between poetry and philosophy is the fragment. It is there that the un-wholly spirit dwells.

Somewhere in his Cantos Ezra Pound says: 'I brought you this crystal ball. Who can lift it?' Plato and Hegel brought us the crystal ball of philosophy. However whereas from a distance its surface looks smooth, the closer you move towards it the more you realize that it is covered by myriad pieces of the broken glass of history. To lift it you must be prepared not only to sink under its weight but also to bleed. Perhaps thinking is bleeding.

Mind is the seeking of salvation in the gathering of love.

On the plane of the death of the gathering an unfolding unfolds: speculative logic.

Everything is contaminated, except the death of the gathering.

As dispersed the private self is many. As gathered, the self belonging to the gathering, is one.

The pulsating gathering is the syllogism of syllogism.

The fundamental teaching of speculative philosophy is that philosophy emerges in a philosophical world. The awareness involved in this teaching is always the result of a dwelling that doesn't involve choice. The thinker is like the sound a stone makes when thrown in the lake marking the beginning of a process that measures the depth of the deep by becoming it. Philosophy is the deepening of the deep, the intensifying of the intense. It is dwelling in a philosophical world. Hegel refers to the dwelling of consciousness in 'pure self recognition in absolute otherness' as the precondition for the initiation of philosophy. Heidegger's Da-sein encounters itself as the questioner situated in the question of being. A dwelling then isn't chosen but received as already received. Does this mean that the thinker cannot escape his given place of dwelling? In so far as thinking involves embracing and permeating what-already-embraces-and-permeates, it intensifies what is already a (philosophical) intensifying. This opens up the possibility of a collapse and thus of the emerging of another, more original, dwelling. The thinker becomes a thinker by accepting and surviving in what survives. Ultimately it is in and out of such fundamental dwellings that a thinker encounters other thinkers. Isn't this what both Hegel and Heidegger teach?

In the death of the gathering: love-madness-vision.

Concepts are visionary ghosts.

What is philosophy? Dwelling in spaces where the defeat of spirit is impossible.

The other side of madness is speculative logic; in between, death.

Poetry, the moment of immediacy, the instance of the everything of everything, belongs to the past. But the past belongs to the future and philosophy is the vision of the future in the past.

Fragments are repetitions of the end, the summary of history from its beyond.

The poet is *necros*. The philosopher is *necrophilos*, the poet and the rebel, dead and the lover of death. But the poet in the rebel is the visionary of love.

The philosopher writes on his empty palm the absence of the poet.

A book of philosophy, what is it? It is the dead body of the gathering-we having the vision of love, the vision of re-gathering itself—the dead body thinking. Thinking is the vision of re-gathering and it becomes this vision by gathering concepts. Is there such a book? Perhaps, after Plato's *Republic*, Hegel's *Science of Logic*.

We are condemned to be the bearers of the idea(l). It is another way of saying that the primordial wor(l)d of philosophy is 'we'.

At one and the same time the poet in me sinks and the rebel in me flies. The rebel encounters himself in the poet in whom the vision is drowned. The poet encounters himself in the rebel and becomes philosopher, the bearer of the vision of vision. Being this tension the ego falls in love with both. Fragments are the forgotten whispers of such falling.

Concepts cry for justice.

The philosopher cultivates concepts in the landscape of *Thanatos*, that of the retreat of the gathering.

The speculative gathering is not only what withstands its complete realization by reviving the command to gather out of itself but also what survives its complete emptiness that the falling in silence of the command produces. The power of the gathering is manifested by this active denying since, far from being destroyed by it, the gathering creates a historically teleological world through this denial and gives rise to the emergence of philosophy as absolute self-knowing. Historically, the gathering manifests itself as 'pure self-recognition' in the 'absolute otherness' of the concept/being emptying out—the *kenosis* of *kenosis*. It is in a philosophical world, in this sense of engagement in active dying, that the place is created for the emergence of philosophy. What is denied, namely the primordial idea of the command/receiving of the gathered gathering-we retreats in the being of the philosopher whose receiving activates the thinking of the universal and indeterminate gathering-we. This thinking, as the thinking of the universal (thought), is the gathering of concepts together with the concept of gathering. It is the singular that 'has the vision of itself as universal', the thinker who realizes the vision conceptually and, ultimately, invokes the idea of history to become reconciled with the actual world that denies the vision. When it is in the world as philosophical in this sense, philosophy gives shape both to the very notion of the philosophical, notion-less actuality of the present as well as to the fulfilled notion of the future.

To think the concept (or to let the concept think you) is to experience death in all its force.

That which leads to love passes through death, which is to say through history.

As he drowns in the infinite retreat of the gathering-we, the poet is transformed into the vortex that recalls all the words of all actual and possible languages, and ultimately language itself, from the world. The world is thus transformed into a wordless world, and the word into a world-less word. Such a recall is the uttering of the 'we' by breathing in (try it). 'We' is the last word, that of the imploding being of the poet. It is also the first word, that of philosophy. Philosophy is the vision of the gathering-we unfolding in the embracing of a death that is always poetic. The death of the visionless poet is inseparable from the visionary philosopher of death.

The philosopher always arrives at the end to gather the broken pieces of the world.

After Hegel and the death of the poet, philosophers can only be the gatherers of whispers (concepts) of the gathering.

When the poet arrived God died. When the poet died the philosopher arrived. In the death of the philosopher the future of the future was announced.

Hegel is Plato resurrected. The second coming has been accomplished.

The retreating gathering is the retreating of language itself. In such a creative act, language becomes world-less as does the world become word-less. Here we have the space in which poetry creates the vision of poeticity. Ultimately, away from any illusions of confessionalism or objectivism, the poet's longing is to whisper the self's implosion, as we do when we farewell our loved ones the moment we are dying or migrating to a foreign land.

We are Wor(l)d-less

our afternoon walks
contain a secret haste
which our pace belies

we greet concealed children
playing with earth and water

and we hope that our distant friend
has not forgotten that pain

pain and memory are now one
the wherewithal for creation of the world

'i want to visit the island of exile' said i
'yes' you replied 'we must observe serenely'

'it's because i love you' i went on
'that i measure the greyness'

shades of that greyness hung from our fingers
in the integrity of the grey beyond
while the landscape had no memory
in its self-admiration

('Twentieth Century', translation from the Greek)

Poets leave the world forever. Philosophers perpetually return. They return in their return. No one is there to welcome them. They will be welcomed by the gathering of the future. Plato is the first to teach us this.

Since those who gather encounter themselves as already gathered, gatherings always precede those who gather in them. That I am as gathered, comes before me. Gatherings then can never be reduced to gatherings of individuals. Individuality is one way of being as gathered in a gathering and of receiving the command to gather. The subjectivity of the individual is this receiving as the already received in the gathering and, as this receiving, subjectivity is the vision of the infinite expansion of its infinite singularity—the becoming of a gatherer. As this receiving of the command to gather, the subject receives the gathering-we by providing it with the notion of the gathering. Ultimately it is this singular receiving that activates the commanding of the command and so itself commands the command to command. It is as the bearer of the universality of the notion of the gathering-we that the subject 'in his particularity has the vision of himself as the universal'. The gathering thus gathers as a project or vision in the *topos* that its own notion is. This *topos* is in turn supplied by the subjectivity of the subject, that is, as Hegel puts it, by the 'I' that is 'thought as a thinker'. Here the 'I' is the house of the visionary 'we'. Accordingly, the gathering-we is the absolute object and the subject is the absolute ego that is embraced in the mutual act of 'unbounded love'. 'That the object [...] is itself universal, permeating and encompassing the ego, also signifies that the pure ego is the pure form which overlaps the object and encompasses it'.

'Everything beautiful is dangerous'
(Kostas Vassilacopoulos).

The reactivation of speculative philosophy will start from fragments like a fire from sparks.

Speculative concepts rise from the pores of the skin, that of the poet.

If the gathering-we happens as absolute power it also happens as love. Hegel speaks of 'free power' as 'free love' and 'boundless blessedness'. The poetic word insists that 'whatever we don't love does not exist' or that 'we dwell, not where we are, but where we love'. As love, the gathering-we is perhaps not only the axiomatic starting point of philosophy but also of communal life itself, as well as their point of return. Moreover, in the absoluteness of its all-embracing aloneness, the happening of the gathering-we is potentially global. That is, in its opening the whole world gathers as the gathering that it is in this most powerful of openings that the gathering-we is. Everything, nature included, is thus a form of gathering that emerges as such in the gathering-we. The being and the very idea of gathering become an issue in so far as the gathering-we gathers its own gathering by dispersing and embracing its dispersal and in doing so posits the mutual informing of being and notion as a project to be realized. This process of gathering is its infinite power, the aloneness that is perfect and the (hidden) source of any vision of perfection (including Plato's).

The philosopher is the dead poet rising.

Thoughts are either the gathering of stars, like a galaxy, or they are not much at all. They let darkness go through them just as the gathering of stars lets the cosmic abyss shine. You never know if this abyss is an explosion or an implosion. Possibly it moves infinitely in both directions, creating the illusion of immobility. Is this illusion what philosophers have called the eternal? The abyss is the retreated gathering whose darkness shines through the concepts of Hegel's *Science of Logic*.

The abyss rises when the gathering implodes.

Philosophy is the principle of rebirth of the gatherer and therefore the most intense death of the gathered possible.

Thinking happens as the thinking of pure thought precisely because it cannot think its purity. Thinking is the unconditional act of the 'cannot'. It is precisely because thinking cannot think that it becomes the impossible act of thinking, that is, of gathering itself. That is why thinking takes place without the imperialism of concepts, since concepts refer to the 'can'.

Thinking must think and not think at one and the same time.

Once I heard the sound the wings of a moth were making as it was trying to move beyond the glass of my window. The sound was like a gathering of whispers. It was a barely audible mystery. I was reminded of Ezra Pound's 'to have heard the farfalla gasping as towards a bridge over worlds'. When I watched carefully I realized what was happening. Behind the window, up in the night sky, the full moon was shining in its majestic aloneness. The moth was trying to reach the moon.

Heidegger lost the way because he found his path.

How and where does one encounter a thinker and what could the meaning of such an encounter be? It is rather obvious that the public acceptance of a thinker as influential, or as a canonical member of the tradition, offers a view from afar, not an encounter. In the philosophically achieved encounter the thinker speaks for the second time. In a sense he revisits his own conceptual place in history now equipped with the wisdom that history itself is. And such wisdom is a remembering of what the initial attempt had forgotten. Perhaps the encounter with a thinker has something to do with the anamnesis of the platonic soul. Through the encounter the thinker remembers. According to Hegel, without being aware of it the philosophical tradition practiced philosophy as the gathering of concepts, the gathering of the thinking of gathering. Gathering is the double act of creating and receiving. What the great philosophers produced was as great as the absence of the properly explicit philosophical element in them. The task of any genuine encounter with the heroes of the pantheon of thought is to make them philosophical. From this perspective 'Hegel' becomes the place of happening of philosophy in its entirety, past, present, and future. Hegel is the supreme gatherer of concepts and consequently the only gatherer of philosophers. In his own way Heidegger attempts something similar. It is the event of thinking itself that makes it necessary for him to (re)visit the ghostly places of his predecessors and speak on their behalf in a voice which would sound strange to the philologist.

Philosophers today must rediscover the intensity of the speculative concept and the integrity of the poem.

The ego is the interiority of the gathering. The gathering is the exteriority of the ego.

Greeks–aloneness: Christians-loneliness.

After Hegel the age longs for a book of philosophy no longer than a few pages.

The gathering is the immobility of the alone.

In the immobility of the alone we gather and disperse beyond time and eternity.

Today it is commonplace for philosophers to throw away the One, like some useless rack. But the decision alone is not enough to throw it away; one must first lift it. Who can lift the One?

Mikis Theodorakis, a great composer of countless pieces on love, revolution, sorrow, and hope, once said that he sometimes felt his works to be like little boats travelling the Mediterranean Sea and not too far off the coast. He had the dark suspicion that the great oceans of music were further out, beyond his reach. Are there any philosophers today suffering from a similar dark suspicion about their own work?

The gathering-we is the 'voyage into the open, where nothing is below or above us, and we stand in solitude with ourselves alone'.

Is it arrogant to claim that one dwells where great thinkers dwelt? Compared to the arrogance of the commentator who judges everything from afar the honesty of such a claim is humility itself. Remaining at a secure distance, we can only hope to sketch the external outline of the temple. We can never experience the dread of dwelling in the temple and in the aloneness of such dwelling.

From the top of Golgotha, while looking down at the unfolding of the past and future centuries, the philosopher stuttered with agony: 'ww…ee, ww…ee' - the first of all words. He thus transformed himself into the only place in which the gathering-we might be gathered, like the sound the afternoon church bell makes, filling the horizon. Hearing him from the bottom of the mountain, the analytic thinker called for a convincing argument. But it is the showing that argues, not the argument that shows. Wasn't this Plato's great contribution?

Poetry is speaking while drowning. Philosophy is practicing your silence whilst dead.

The justice of the concept is the inner.

There are three categories of philosophers around. There are those who think the aim of philosophy is to teach us how to die; and those who think that philosophy is worth its name if it shows us how to live. Then there are those who are obsessed with puzzles. In other words, philosophers today do little more than exorcise the practice of death, the only *askesis* that makes one into a philosopher, that is, lover.

The tragedy of the era: in our saying, nothing is said; and in our said, there is no saying.

The only ego that cannot utter the word 'we' is God. And 'God' is the only word that, as gatherer, the ego need not utter.

The speculative notion is the bearer of death.

Those who haven't reached the destination cannot think since thinking is always a return. Philosophizing is moving backwards. The gathering of philosophers is the gathering of returns without turns. It is a coming back from the future of redemption. It is a coming back, however, that never has a future. Once arrived, the philosopher permanently dwells amongst those with no memory of the vision.

Poets never return. They only dwell in the destination they've already reached. That is why the poet doesn't need the philosopher whereas the philosopher needs the poet. Don't philosophize if you aren't a poet. However, without the philosopher the poet only despairs, since he is unable to return. To find yourself at the destination is a blessing, a gift of some kind. To dwell in it without the possibility of returning is a curse. Poets are blessed and cursed. The resolution of this antinomy is the non-resolution of a personal death.

Philosophers pretend that death is dead.

To paraphrase the poet: 'I loved them as philosophers love the thinking that kills them, as drowned sailors the sea.' What is the use of a philosophy that doesn't kill?

It is the snake that is at once poet and philosopher. The poet in the snake is the shedding of the skin. The philosopher is the growing of the new skin out of the exposed flesh. Both involve, not wonder, but the agony of love. That is why Plato is closer to us than Aristotle. With Aristotle the poet in the philosopher was lost.

Why is Speculative philosophy a system? Because death can only be systemic, at once embracing and permeating.

A speculative concept is the landscape of death. A concept is like a place abandoned by glorious gatherings. It is there that the soul of the philosopher dwells. The philosopher is the memory of the gathering. That is why we never read philosophy books to understand. We read them in order to encounter the soul remembering in the landscape of death.

The speculative absolute proves itself when it dies.

We never encounter individuals. That we encounter individuals as individuals is a fiction of liberalism. We encounter worlds, that is, places of gatherings. A world is always a world of worlds. Because worlds repeat themselves in the being of each member of the gathering, to destroy a world you need mass killings. This is the story of the twentieth century. Hate of the other is hate of another world. But liberal individualism is the hate of the world as such.

Can liberalism survive without destroying the world in us? Liberalism is a vampire that sucks the life-blood from worlds.

When the philosopher leaves the city he takes the gathering-we with him. What are left behind are blind persons arguing over who sees more clearly. Amongst them many claim to be philosophers.

In the village of philosophers how does one differentiate between the tourist and the local?

The philosopher is beyond being lost or forgotten. He simply cannot be found by those who look for him, like birds of prey. Hegel is the prime example.

Like a giant, philosophy travels from one mountain peak to the next. Those in the valley confuse the shadow of philosophy for philosophy itself.

At one and the same time everything moves towards the great end and the even greater beginning. These have been announced by Hegel, the only thinker who uttered the 'we'. He listened from afar to the coming of the gathering.

A philosopher speaks by remaining hidden. If you find him he'll fall into silence. Because remaining hidden is what matters, it makes no difference whether the philosopher is alive or dead.

The world engages with lovers. It is love that the world cannot resist. If we replace 'thinking' with 'love' we might be able to appreciate why Hegel insisted that the world cannot resist the power of reason. But usually philosophers know very little about love and its command: Those of you who are wordless, be as a world.

In philosophy we sometimes fall in love with a title first and then decide to write a book. From this perspective, writing a book is a matter of staying with the title for as long as possible.

A dispersed body is the precondition for philosophy, because philosophy is the gathering of the gathering out of the most radical dispersing. But who can survive such an event and such a view?

The dispersed ones are neighbours. The gathered ones are lovers. Don't be a neighbour to your lover.

I was surprised to find out how many philosophers wear ties. Or is it the tie that wears the philosopher?

Hegel says that selves throw light upon each other. So far in history this has been announced by those who set themselves alight for justice and freedom. The philosopher must also be prepared to set oneself alight by the vision of justice. Concepts are flames of vision. Hegel's *Science of Logic* is a gathering of flames bearing the vision of justice.

True philosophers have palms that carry flames.

Put your head in a well, and you'll scream. The emergence of Wor(l)ds presupposes such screaming.

The creation of concepts presupposes their justice has been fulfilled.

'And if we don't die for each other we are already dead.' (Tasos Livaditis) Philosophy is the lamenting of not being in a position to die for the other.

Philosophy is euthanasia or it is nothing. But only the dead can will to die their death. How can someone desire something he is not?

The only thing that is 'beyond' thinking is thought— the universality of the indeterminate gathering-we. Thinking is embracing, activated by uttering: 'we'. The 'clearing' for thinking is the indeterminate gathering, infinite love, in which the philosopher is already situated as gathered. Thinking presupposes being infinitely passive, as loved.

Only the unbearable can bear us. And only through such bearing can we bear it. But the unbearable is the infinite love of the indeterminate gathering-we. As loved, we become lovers of the unbearable.

Plato knew that one becomes a philosopher by facing the possibility of annihilation when encountering the light of perfection, the infinite integrity of presencing. Isn't this the experience of the one who moves out of the cave? The painful process culminates in facing the Sun and thus the possibility of blindness. To regain vision out of the possibility of blindness is the act presupposed by thinking. It is through such an act that one is really thrown in the realm of the forms.

With the emergence of Hegel's speculative philosophy history ended. It was also released as that which is ending. What is the end of history, the end of the procession of forms, if not the release of the indeterminate gathering-we, and who is the speculative philosopher, if not the one who bears the principle and the conceptual vision of such gathering? The very idea of the end of history appears when such ending has already begun. The democratization of the being of the philosopher will occur at its completion since everyone will act philosophically, as the place of dwelling of the gathering.

The embrace of the philosopher is empty. The philosopher appears when everyone has already left. But the true philosopher insists on embracing the emptiness of this embracing.

Only as embracing and as embraced can we not-be.

The revolutionary has the vision of the new world. This is the vision of forms, of gatherings, and structures. The philosopher has the vision of the vision. This is the vision of the primordial, the indeterminate gathering-we, the rebel of the perpetual rebellion. When the revolutionary retreated, the philosopher appeared. Philosophy is the revolution reclaiming itself from itself—the wisdom of the night.

The rebellion in the indeterminate gathering is its stasis, its rebellious immobility.

What is the difference between God's love and the love of the indeterminate gathering-we? God's is the love needed by the lonely, the empty ego of the property owner. The love of the gathering is the infinity of our aloneness.

First the embrace, then the face.

The embrace is the expansion of the face. The face is the contraction of the embrace. This is the pulse of the pulsating ego.

The one who believes that politics has nothing to do with love practices love in terms of politics: the temporary alliance of the two.

(French Revolution) + (Plato) = Hegel
(Hegel) - (French Revolution) = Nietzsche
(French Revolution) - (Hegel) = Marx
(0) - (Hegel) = 20th century thought

Evil is more radical than nothing. Being the doers of evil we are beyond the question 'why is there something rather than nothing?'

God emerges in the depths of the formal ego's emptiness. The philosophical example of this is Descartes. The ego, which as gathered gathers the gathering, the fulfilled by the gathering ego, fulfilling itself as the gatherer of the gathering, needs no God.

In the depths of God's love we can detect hate for the gathering, since the gathering is the creator of the divine. It is this hate that the organized church expresses.

Nietzsche was right about the Christian herd. But he was right for the wrong reasons.

Plato understood that what determines the character of the Good is the gathering. He avoided a hateful God by experiencing the Good as indifferent. A divinity that loves us would also hate us because of its dependence on us. We would then have to blame ourselves, as sinners, for such hate.

Only a member of the herd can hate the herd like Nietzsche does.

Christians gather around their dead as around someone who departs forever in the beyond of this life. Revolutionaries gather around their dead heroes to claim them as eternal places of dwelling for the gathering of the here and now. Names of heroes and martyrs are places where the indeterminate gathering gathers as the bearer of the vision of the gathering. Let's not Christianize our dead heroes by saying farewell to them.

We can speak of the dead gathering only with a dead language.

Only in revolutions can we get a glimpse of the energy of redemption generated by the indeterminate gathering, which cancels history as the procession of forms.

Even so it is impossible for us even to imagine the power of affirmation of the indeterminate gathering that the collapse of history will release. The indeterminate gathering will be the only true poet of life, the shaper and the creator.

All those philosophers who talk about the value of a rational dialogue are polite egoists who think they are the bearers of the ultimate state of humanity. The issue is not the clarity of communication but the event of the communal gathering of visionaries. Not the discipline of argument but the disorientation of redemption offered by the indeterminate gathering-we will take us to the beyond of every violence by making us absolutely passive, speechless receivers of the Yes.

Affirmation is the only violence that destroys the world of oppression by cancelling itself.

Initially it is history that will release the indeterminate gathering as the destroyer of forms and thus of history itself. What will spring from this rebellion is platonic Justice, perpetually releasing the indeterminate gathering and perpetually arising from it.

There is only one philosophical title: The Gathering. And only one book of philosophy, that of the gathering. That is why any true philosophy is a re-writing of *The Republic*, whose title might have been 'The

Gathering'. Isn't this the case with Hegel's *Spirit* as well?

Let's not confuse the historical with history. The historical is what belongs to a linear process of constellations of forms cancelling and succeeding each other. History is the spatial co-existence of all forms—the formal universality of particularity (Toula Nicolacopoulos). The historical is linear succession: history is implosion, the implosion of time itself, its transformation into space.

The ever-increasing speed associated with technological efficiency is time transforming itself into space.

Capitalism is time having the vision of itself as space.

In the Ethical State of gathering, what would release the releasing of the command to gather? How would the process of return to the indeterminate gathering be activated? These aren't trivial questions because they refer directly to the possibility of perpetual rebellion.

The most radical rebellion starts after the rebels have established their justice.

The gathering-we is the justice of justice. We know this since Plato.

In the indeterminate gathering of the future the intensity of the Greek Dionysian will be like a drop in the ocean. Compared to the determinate gathering of the future, the majesty of the Greek Apollonian will fade like an autumn leaf.

Speculative history, the procession of forms, is never a linear process. From the beginning it is an implosion—the slow transformation of time into space. In its latest phase history is the implosion of the implosion. Form and content come together in a deadly embracing. The end result will be the release of the indeterminate, pure significance.

Historical time is a falling into where we already are—in the stillness of the indeterminate gathering. Such falling deepens the deep.

Only in a philosophical world can philosophy be activated as the desire of the gatherer for redemption.

When you look at the world with empty eyes the world looks back at you emptily, with the eyes of a skull. It is precisely then that God emerges as the saviour of the impotent. That was Descartes' experience.

The gathering is more than its notion and more than its being. But it is this more as notion and as being.

Therefore the gathering overflows itself. But as this overflowing it falls into itself, like the waterfall that falls into the river.

In the indeterminacy of the indeterminate gathering everything breaks down. Even the breaking down breaks down. It is then that the vision arises.

The issue isn't communication, but community. To employ language doesn't mean to open oneself to the force of the better argument. It means to be the bearer of the vision of the gathering-we, to be a mind. Language isn't a bridge but the place of visionary dwellings. In order to reach the place we have to destroy the bridges.

The 'we' is the pure encounter. Only by encountering the encounter can we encounter each other.

What legitimizes a philosophy is its rhythm, the rhythm concepts make when they arise. What legitimizes a poem is equally its rhythm, the rhythm words make when they fall.

The challenge of humanity is to reconcile itself with itself. This is the lesson taught by speculative philosophy.

No matter where or when or how, our condition is that of gathering. Our gathering takes place in the gathering. The gathering commands us to gather. In receiving the command we disperse essentially as dispersing in order to re-gather.

We are already in the gathering, with a misunderstanding of the gathering.

Philosophy is activated in the battlefield that the self of the philosopher is, once this self is determined by the power to think of itself as that which has the power to disrupt the pure formalism of subjectivity and thereby to point to something more fundamental. This is a disruption in history itself since history is constituted as the dispersed gathering of property owners. Through this disruption the eternal invades history in a manner that renders it impossible for history to resist. In other words, the retreating event determines philosophy as its truth process that directly intervenes in history by thinking it. Ultimately only an event without an evental site posits the very idea of commanding to which philosophy responds. History is the situation of the event that does not depend on a site. Here, what is to be thought is not an object but the significance for the world of the very possibility of philosophy, since history is created through the presupposition of this very possibility. As Hegel notes, history is the emptying out of Spirit, that is, of the gathering-we. What we have here is the in-principle implosion of the world that releases the very idea of the gathering-we, an idea fully realized as philosophy.

As revolution the gathering reveals and retreats. Then it awaits itself at the end of history.

Only the coming gathering can save us.

When everyone will have the experience of the immanent end of everything, including the end itself, the beginning will arrive.

The command to gather will be activated through the implosion of the world. Out of deafness the most sensitive listening will be produced.

The world is a child of love, that of the indeterminate gathering with the gathered ones.

The one who receives is the one who is blessed by the universal blessing of the indeterminate gathering.

The gathering-we posits the philosopher as the one who makes possible the happening of its retreat as this retreat. The fact of the retreat, what is already a fact, also happens, through philosophy. Therefore philosophy always comes late in order to recollect the retreat, to make it happen, and thus to reveal its meaning. The philosopher embraces the retreat and through this embracing the significance of the retreat is revealed in visionary terms.

The philosopher practices the thinking receiving that receives.

Modernity is self- posited as the perpetual present, the present that floods the future.

Marx tried to restore the future in the present, but not through the indeterminate gathering. Therefore the enemy was the structures of capitalism not the dispersing of property owners. It was then inevitable for him to try to locate the agent of revolution in those structures. And it was inevitable that the revolutionary form, emerging in the land of dispersion, could only be developed around the ethical principle of democratic centralism (Lenin).

We shouldn't try to understand property ownership through capitalism but capitalism through property ownership. Property ownership is older than capitalism. Any crisis in capitalism, no matter how deep, is never deep enough since it never disturbs property ownership. The only thing that could disturb it is the coming of the indeterminate gathering.

By turning the ethical universalism of the future into the past, the nation-state emerges.

Capitalist crises are stations in the ever-increasing intensification of exchange. The materiality of capital is created by the ideality of the empty self, the owner. The implosion of the ideal will lead to the indeterminate gathering of minds.

Dispersion disperses by shattering the bonding of the indeterminate gathering to come. Because it negates the indeterminate gathering it negates the future. It divides the indeterminate from the determinate. The indeterminate that doesn't give rise to form as an act of freedom is the gathering of dispersion.

The first philosopher to pray was Plato, since praying is the gathering of concepts in the aloneness of mind. It is out of such aloneness that the command 'know thyself' emerges.

In the Platonic dialogues Socrates acts not as an interlocutor but as a place of dwelling for his friends.

The historical result of the abandonment of God is the universalism of property ownership. The 'everyone is equal before God' is replaced by our radical equality before the thing owned. The thing and our relation to it become the most radical expression of the abandonment of our aloneness and the positing of our loneliness. We are offered being, not by the 'I' who can say 'We' but by the thing. In order for us to dwell, everything must be transformed into the dwelling place that the Thing is. The thing (ful)fills our loneliness.

What the empty self sees in the world is its own emptiness. The empty self is the emptying of the empty world.

The empty empties emptiness emptily.

Emptiness is perfect. The emptiness of the empty self shines emptily.

The empty self is empty of world.

The thing owned is the boat of the empty self in the sea of emptiness.

The voice of being is the silence of the concept.

The gathering-we accommodates an infinite number of voices by being one silence. Listening to the silence of the gathering is the only true listening.

The empty self is the dark sense of the speculative gathering. It is the awareness of something missing.

In the things to be owned and as owned, the property owner finds no resistance. He moves around and between them freely, that is, aimlessly. He moves around in his moving around as the gatherer of things and the destroyer of worlds.

In the beyond of things owned, the owner encounters himself as the hedonism of his insignificance.

In the thing owned I am infinitely lonely. In what gives me being I am already absent. How strange to depart the very moment I arrive.

In the thing I own my insignificance stares at me. The thing offers me being by taking significance away from me.

The singularity of the owner is expressed through the infinite exclusion of all others from what he owns. In so far as he truly is the owner no one can come from the present, the past, or the future, or from another place anywhere in the universe, and claim it as his property. Therefore they all gather in the thing I own as excluded from it. The thing then becomes the *topos* of my exile.

Only those who systematize can fragmentize. Nietzsche does neither.

I don't encounter the other; I dwell in the other.

Freedom or death: it is the love of the gathering that makes this choice, the only choice we have, possible.

The thing-in-itself cannot be known, it can only be owned. Kant was partly right. Speculative philosophy starts from what he missed.

The law of asymmetry mediates between me and the thing that I own. The thing is the power that makes my singularity insignificant by making me replaceable.

Once you get rid of the mediating property item, the other becomes the one who arrives indefinitely. Therefore your only option is to prepare for this arrival by perpetually undermining any form of symmetry that result from the mediating thing. Such preparing isn't an overcoming but another expression of enacting the emptiness of the self.

As owned, the thing permeates my emptiness and overflows it, thus positing itself as the place of my dwelling.

With the exception of Hegel, philosophy from Descartes to Heidegger will one day be judged on its inability to theorize what is fundamental for the entire age: owning.

Once the ego is empty of the notion—the ego is this emptiness—it can only think, unthinkingly. The scientist is a prime example.

Stripped of the notion, the ego is abstractly singular; not the gatherer but the liberator of concepts; one who can do no more than deconstruct. As merely singular and non-expanding, the ego can enter any conceptual system undetected.

Derrida concentrates on that which is encountered. In doing so he postpones the encounter.

We are already in the encounter as encountered and encountering. The encounter doesn't have a 'before' and an 'after'.

Can philosophy be a latecomer? Can philosophy come too late to be instructive for philosophers?

The law of nature holds: from birth to death. The law of the spirit holds: from death to birth. Life is what matters for nature, whereas for spirit it is the integrity of vision.

Philosophy arrives at the point at which the world is furthest from itself.

As owned the thing gives being to the already deceased.

The empty self oscillates between a scientific and a religious explanation of the genesis of the gathering. The disagreement here is a family feud.

No matter where you go in Greece, the Greek landscape, urban or not, is haunted by history. It is the landscape of ruins, the traces left behind by great gatherings, which once dreamed of eternity and possibly even of themselves as eternal. Not only people and their creations but even nature itself emerges out of these ever present ruins. Do these monumental fragments refer us to the past, or do they point to our future? Or do they position us in our present as the perpetual technology of ruins and fragments? Possibly that which differentiates us from past civilizations is the fact that we don't create in order to enable time to destroy. We create our world as the world of ruins, of dismemberment, and out of this we release time from its traditional role of being the executioner of magnificent worlds. It is now the servant of an a priori *pathos* for self-mutilation. We've already prepared what the peoples of the future will receive from us, by already presenting ourselves to ourselves as history itself in immediate and direct action. Possibly modern art is at the forefront of this.

The vision is fully embraced when one has lost all hope. Christianity is the converse.

The philosopher returns to the cave to announce. The force of his announcement is expressed by the fact that he is unlike those still in the cave. This is the proof of the other world of which he is the bearer. The challenge to the others isn't to become like him by exiting the cave, but to re-gather *in him*. Such a re-gathering constitutes their radical transformation and the proof of the existence of this other reality.

The philosopher escapes from the cave as a prisoner without a prisoner escaping with him.

Derrida is the Other who has arrived. His deconstruction is his vision of being welcomed, or his despair of not being welcomed. Derrida is the philosopher that greets himself.

Only a world can save us.

The self is at once 'impenetrable' and fully exposed to the other. It encounters itself at the edge of this antithesis.

The self that longs for the other is the self that has already made the other homeless.

When the empty self turns against itself and its world it moves towards the speculative that has been abandoned by the world. Since in doing so it is still the empty self it also moves away from the speculative towards itself; it is unable to escape the world. Its oscillating relation with the speculative is thus one of love/hate. Is this what defines philosophy after Hegel?

If the philosopher conflates his own critique with the event of the destruction of the world and then waits, the world never arrives.

God dies many times over in our private selves.

Every philosopher who situates himself outside the speculative loses the world and in doing so takes himself to have arrived before the world, whether as liberator, or as a prophet. Here the speculative order is reversed. Instead of appreciating the speculative of the world as that which implodes into its own beyond by releasing its vision, the philosopher conflates his derivative scepticism with such implosion. Consequently he doesn't think of himself as a response and radical outcome of the world's radicality. He rather thinks of himself as a radical doing and then the question becomes whether the world will be able to follow his philosophy. Of course, no definite answer can be given here simply because the world 'refuses' to be addressed by such thinking.

Nietzsche never managed to transform the world into a vision because he never managed to transform himself into a world.

The world moves not from but towards its origin. The origin of the world is the result of an arrival. History is the implosion of the gathering towards its origin, a moving backward, leading to the division and thus to an infinite intensification of spirit through which spirit releases itself as the self-releasing. The movement of implosion takes place in the infinite immobility of the gathering. Being immobile means the gathering waits for itself to arrive and only by making its waiting infinite does spirit arrive. Spirit returns as returning but as this returning, spirit is also a moving away.

Return is activated when spirit reaches the furthest from itself—its absolute otherness, death.

One day philosophy will be judged according to its power not to shed light but to bear darkness. The philosopher is the bearer of darkness having the vision of light.

The pre-condition for philosophy is the body that the gathering has loved but has also abandoned. This is the 'Hegel' body, the body of the gatherer. Once abandoned, the head without body appears.

The gathering is the lover of the body.

How is darkness generated if not by the implosion of the gathering? The gathering falls into itself, it implodes under its own weight. Out of its darkness it reveals itself as everything—the whole. Then the dancing commences.

To embrace or not to embrace?

History is a succession of intensities of significance.

Christians sought God because he had arrived. Kierkegaard sought God because he left.

What does the thinker see on the edge of the gathering? The gathering exploding and imploding. From the edge of the gathering the gathering emerges as the pulsating abyss.

The ego is the desire to empty itself of emptiness. The divine springs from such desire.

The 'same' is that which returns as returning. In that case it is also a moving away and therefore an-already having-arrived in the place from which it returns. But the place in which it arrives is the arriving of the place itself. It arrives as arriving. Arriving is then the place. You arrive in the arriving. In arriving as arriving you return as returning. You cannot arrive without returning, and you cannot be as returning without also being as arriving.

The only way to encounter oneself is to move away and to return simultaneously.

The ego is the singular, which is also the all-embracing vision of the gathering. The ego is at one and the same time moving away and coming back.

Historical time doesn't move forward but backwards towards its source of activation. Historical time is implosion and therefore time contracts as it approaches its absolute limit. Time isn't elastic. It is a deepening, a search within itself for its source, the indeterminate gathering.

That which implodes, explodes. History is the condensing that also expands.

We think when we cannot sing the song of the gathering. From this perspective philosophy is the singing silence.

In the future the world will fit in to a small song.

Philosophy is always a night song.

The world that is for us unbearable and that the philosopher is condemned to bear, will be a plaything to the children of the future.

The Stoics, the Epicureans, the neo-Platonists, all of them dwelt in the space between the Platonic idea and the Christian practice of the gathering. Because of this they had neither the memory of the gathering that was left behind nor the vision of the gathering that was arriving. All of them were anti-Platonic in the deepest and most radical sense.

Thinking is the joy of the dead.

In order to see the world change you have to be strong enough to dwell in your own extinction.

The first to struggle against the Christian gathering was Plato, the seer of the past.

Socrates was Socrates. Plato was the becoming of Socrates.

In its full manifestation the speculative gathering is the self-realizing realized world of gathering. It is the realized gathering that does not sink into the fullness of its realization only to become inert. As fully realized the gathering retrieves the indeterminate gathering without destroying what it has realized. The gathering is thus the visionary power and process of return and projection. It returns to itself as the agent of indeterminacy out of which the gathering is released as the already realized project. It is the releasing of the already released. As the power of releasing its world the gathering is also powerful enough not to be lost in the radical abyss of its indeterminacy. Out of its indeterminacy it posits its world as the world that has already been realized and as the world that retrieves its realizing. In the gathering's pulsating movement between the realized gathering and the formless gathering the world perpetually opens itself to the eternal command to 'be as a world', that is, to be as the world that is posited in and by the retrieving of the command. As this kind of movement of absolute negativity the absolute manifests as the power to formulate the gathering in terms of the project of the co-belonging of notion and being as well as the realizing realized realization of such co-belonging. Absolute negativity is the pulsating world of the absolute. It is the aloneness of the gathering-we.

'To live like an immortal': Is this really the challenge? The challenge is the impersonal death of the gathering. Only the one who knows how to actually practice this kind of death becomes the bearer of the eternal Idea. Immortality is a form of practicing mortality, the dead one thinking.

Philosophy has nothing to do with living life. When the philosopher arrives life has already departed. The philosopher is the *necrophilos* consumed by the practice and vision of love.

Stop living and start loving.

Absolute knowing is the agony of the inner. It is the agony of the vision without hope.

Wherever and whenever the speculative realists arrive, the erotic hides its face behind the smoke of ruins.

The challenge is to answer answers without asking questions. Let's make the slave master not by opposing but by singing.

Descartes announced the self in its immobile simplicity. Kant articulated the frozen shapes of such immobility. Fichte tried to energise the self. But the self-energising self is a sound without meaning.

To explain something by treating it as a 'fact' presupposes that one has already submitted to it. Consequently the explanation simply renders explicit the structure of submission. Isn't this the case with Hume's emphasis on habit, and Kant's theory of mind?

Kant's categorical imperative is the cry of the submissive pretending to be free.

I saw myself amongst the dead and cried.

For philosophers today, death is dead. Unfortunately, there are no longer poets around to protest.

The gathering becomes an issue only when those who participate in the realized gathering make an issue of their capacity to be as gathered (and as gatherers) and, relatedly, of their capacity to generate and respond to the very idea of gathering in so far as they recollect themselves as the visionary gathered-to-be. This dual act—recollecting the vision from what is already the vision's realized form and projecting the vision's realization in what is already its realized form—is the pulse of the gathering-we, a pulse 'felt' in all forms of gathering irrespective of their degree of comprehensiveness. So, for example, in falling in love with someone (the elemental gathering of two) one encounters oneself as gathered in the gathering of love, which is also the power to create the world of love. In this primordial sense of the gathering/gathered mutuality of the gathering, the power of the gathering-we takes the form of a command—the command to gather as loving and hence to create the world of love. As already gathered in the gathering of love and hence as already received by love, individuals are the receivers of such a command where the commanding is itself activated in and as this receiving. At the same time, once lovers have created the world of love, they retrieve the command from within it by perpetually (re)enacting their world. So the life of the gathering of love is neither simply the world of love nor is it the indeterminate gathering out of which this world springs. This life is the pulse that makes possible a perpetual return, an embracing of the beginning by the end and of the end by the beginning. The gathering is both anamnesic and visionary in this way and every form of gathering presupposes that it is a response to the command to gather.

Every questioner can turn around and ask: Why should I bother with this question? There is no love in questioning because there is no questioning in love.

The questioner is the lover who lost his vision.

What is the greatest accusation god could make against the philosopher? 'You forgot to practice dying because you forgot to love.'

Philosophy has little to do with teaching one how to live, or with instructing one on how to die. In both cases death is understood as something that belongs to the future. But for the philosopher it is death that is always the place of dwelling of someone who has already died from the intensity of love.

Questioning is nihilism.

The concept is the agony of the mortal.

It is true that life is always impure. But it is equally true that death is absolutely pure. It is the purity of death that the philosopher seeks with all his strength.

The rhythm of the speculative is the breath of death.

The true empiricist is the one who sees nothing.

It is wrong to ask: 'why is there something rather than nothing?' The appropriate question is: 'why is there nothing rather than something?'

The infinity of nature is the simplicity of its indifference.

In order to greet each other we have first to gather the nothingness of nature.

It is true that Socrates is the philosopher who doesn't write. But it is also true that he is the one who gathers. The philosopher who writes is Plato. After the death of Socrates he is the one who dwells in the retreat of the philosophical gathering. By dwelling in such a retreat and thus by becoming the agent through whom the retreat of the gathering happens Plato's thought becomes the articulation of the vision of the gathering and of the philosopher as the gatherer of concepts.

Like the failed revolution that precedes it and makes it possible and necessary as a response to despair, philosophy opens an opening for the future to appear and announce itself for a second time. For this to be achieved the philosopher arrives both too late and too early. Too late because he arrives when everything has already happened; too early because he arrives when the happening has yet to happen. From this perspective Plato is the first philosopher and *The Republic* is the first philosophical text. It wouldn't be unreasonable to suggest that all the other platonic dialogues ought to be read through *The Republic*, or that *The Republic* ought to be read without any substantial reference to any of the other dialogues. It would also not be unreasonable to suggest that as far as philosophy's past is concerned, in order to come to terms with philosophy's history and with history itself the genuine philosophical act is to appropriately retrieve *The Republic*—the original reflective moment on the being and meaning of the gathering-we. History as such emerges by providing us with its text. *The Republic* is the first book of history, the introduction of history into history. However, up until our own era this retrieving has remained a task.

Plato's *Republic* proposes that justice is a matter of knowing one's proper place in the gathering of the *polis*, but what is the proper place of *The Republic* itself? If, as Plato suggests, philosophy can show us what justice is, what is the justice that belongs to philosophy? To what kind of justice does philosophy belong? If indeed there is a proper place in which the dialogue of *The Republic* unfolds, the supreme awareness of such place must already be there from the outset as the supreme itself. And, by extension, there must also be present the awareness of the proper place of, or role performed by, such place. But who would be the bearers of this awareness, in what capacity, and where would they be located? Where would this awareness come from and how would the creator of *The Republic*, Plato himself, be related to this awareness? Perhaps, and in so far as these questions have some legitimacy, answers ought to be given right at the beginning of the dialogue. But if this is indeed the case, and those answers are already available, the activation of philosophy presupposes not questions but the affirmation of what is fundamental. From this perspective the activation of *The Republic* becomes possible and necessary in the light of an already achieved awareness of a primordial orientation. Could it be that this orientation reveals to philosophy the nature of justice as well as the justice of philosophy? Does *The Republic* articulate the becoming of what one already is? The starting point of the text known as *The Republic* is usually considered to consist of Socrates narrating the dialogue to an unspecified audience that is attentive but otherwise silent. But the noteworthy aspect of this audience is that its members must be taken to be already aware of themselves as being in the presence of the philosopher. Their perspective differs to this extent from the ordinary reader of *The Republic*. By contrast, in proceeding to read the dialogue the latter is positioned as the narrator who is unaware of Socrates' role until later in the discussion—unless, of course, the proper reader/narrator of the text happens to be the philosopher himself. So one cannot (properly) read *The Republic* without taking the position of the philosopher as the narrator and hence without being both like Socrates and radically unlike him in so far as one reads *The Republic*. Moreover, if the identification of the narrator with the philosopher is non-contingent, *The Republic* could not have been narrated without the gathering of the appropriate audience—that which exclusively belongs to the philosopher and to which the philosopher exclusively belongs. But if this is indeed what happens, could the silence of the members of the unspecified audience stem from their awareness of being present in the presence of the philosopher? Could their listening be this very silence, a silence the philosopher himself must listen to when he narrates *The Republic* as the place in which his narrating fulfils the mission of reading *The Republic*? Taking into account the idea of an audience positioned as listening silently to the philosopher, their interaction appears to be characterized by a violently erotic mutual informing—the embracing of two antithetical elements, like fire and water, without however destroying each other each being enacted and intensified through the other. The narrator never disturbs the listening (by asking, for example, 'what do you think?'), and the ones who listen do not interrupt the narration (by asking 'what do you mean?'). There is an intermixing that preserves and enhances the purity of the two acts. Purity is here a result, that of contamination. In other words there is a role differentiation, and performances related to this, that are never to be violated. Possibly the silence acquires its form as listening by artfully receiving the narration whose aim it is precisely to let the listening happen. Do those who listen, listen for the first time, by emerging (leaping) through such listening and as this listening? Do we have here the enactment of listening itself? Is their silence a primordial silence, which in its simplicity, or precisely because of its simplicity, is being erotically saturated and thus enhanced by the voice of the philosopher? Is the simplicity and endurance of their silence the infinite and enduring opening to the philosophical voice? Could this mean that the philosopher is the only one with a voice and that he speaks for the first time? Perhaps the philosopher is the one who always speaks for the first time, the time of speaking. But, of course, on this scenario he speaks by reading what Plato, the homeless philosopher who never had the appropriate welcoming audience, has already written. Perhaps in listening silently the members of the audience are not themselves in a position to listen to their own silence. They are not present in themselves. Instead they present themselves in a place that doesn't belong to them and to which they belong in a way that makes it imperatively proper for them to return to and greet themselves as for the first time by traversing its planes. Their silence and hence their listening happens 'out there' where the voice is. The voice of the philosopher becomes the place of dwelling of the silent ones and of their one singular silence. They are individual listeners through their collective silence. They fall into silence and they become listeners the moment they encounter the descending philosopher. For his part the philosopher speaks the moment this silence is enacted through this speaking. Therefore the silent ones are already ecstatic and this is why they are silent beyond their silence—they listen and they are as this listening. In other words, they find themselves in their silence when surrounded by the presence of the philosopher and the power of his voice. (Does the voice of the philosopher have a voice, or is it a voiceless voice given that the philosopher narrates/the voice reads what is written?) Where does this voice come from? Could it be that it comes out of a coming from, that of the descent of the philosopher from the realm of the Good? It is the voice that is activated when the philosopher is welcomed and hence it is the voice that urges towards the Good. So what is initially decisive here is the pure saying of the philosopher and not what is said, that is, what is subsequently said about the ideal of justice. In actual fact once activated the saying of the philosopher doesn't change. It functions as the field within which the said emerges. Such a perpetual and pure saying perpetually requires the 'clean canvas', the indeterminacy of the indeterminate gathering, purely receiving the philosopher as the bearer of the Good. And the Good of course cannot be said; it is pointed to as the urge that the saying is and, by extension, as the collective urge released in the listening and as this listening. The saying is thus presupposed by the said as that which can never itself be said. It is the indeterminacy of the pure saying of the philosopher that functions as the gatherer of the indeterminate gathering. Consequently, the dialogue unfolds in the very act of being narrated and this in a way that affirms the silence of the audience of the philosopher without itself falling into silence. It is enacted in the voice of the one as the one voice embracing and being embraced by the silence of the many as the one silence. Is this silence the proper place of the dialogue and is its proper way of being to be as narrated by the philosopher? And if so, what is the philosophical significance of the narrating if not to shape the perpetually indeterminate gathering of rebels and what is the philosophical significance of the philosopher being the narrator if not to gather the gathering? Given that the narrator is the philosopher, his proper place is to be as the narrator of this great story. In this case, at least in principle, *The Republic* is the only story that a philosopher can narrate to the ecstatic ones—the story of ecstasy and justice. In *The Republic* then we should be able to detect in all its purity and majesty the primordial ambition of philosophy: to create the story of the gathering for the gathering and thus to make the gathering gather itself through the narrating of this story. This vision is philosophically significant because it is the ambition of philosophy itself. It is the only ambition philosophy can have in order to encounter itself *as philosophy*. The proper place of philosophy, philosophy's own justice, is this ambition. Perhaps Plato thought of his *Republic* as that which ought to replace the Homeric epics. Or we might say, to think of Plato as the philosopher is to think of him in terms of such an ambition. For this reason the positioning of the philosopher as the ruler of the city of justice ultimately demonstrates that once the gathering has given itself form by constructing the differentiated order of the just *polis* the indeterminate gathering retains its relevance, as that from which the *polis* perpetually springs, through the narration of *The Republic*. But if this is the case, and the fully developed gathering of the just *polis* is also what perpetually refers itself to the primordial indeterminate gathering, then perhaps in order to capture both these aspects of the being of the gathering we should translate 'Politia' as 'The Gathering'.

The fragment dwells in the place between poetry and philosophy, and it is itself this very place. It is the middle term of a syllogism that mediates between the moving away and the return by moving away and returning.

The gathering is the amassing of intensity in order to irrupt. It is division, the being of the 'NOT', and therefore the infinite recalling of the 'YES'.

Only the NOT can save us.

'we   we   we .....': the ego flashing in the abyss of cosmic darkness.

The French Revolution was the irruption of the indeterminate gathering-we manifesting itself as the imperative: 'be as a world'. In a singular moment that was the moment of the singular it captured the idea of the movement of history as the gathering that gathers itself. In the happening of the infinite aloneness of the indeterminate gathering-we each member of the collective is claimed as the place of dwelling for the other members, as the bearer of the very idea of gathering. Here the subjectivity of the subject is constituted in the inter-relation of expansion, as the embracing of the collective, and contraction, as being absolutely permeated by the substantive universality of solidarity.

It is a certain experience of indeterminacy, of significance, that permits one to observe the gathering of the centuries, past and future, that history is.

From a speculative perspective, instead of the linear progression towards the hegemony of knowledge in the form of the all-encompassing rational state, history is the implosion of gatherings of forms under their own weight, which releases the indeterminate.

Where does history announce itself as the destroyer of the kind of form that is deaf to the calling of the indeterminate and how does the philosopher receive such calling?

Hegel's philosophy, like Plato's before him and unlike any other philosophy after him, is the reception of the last whisper of the eternal command: gather. The receiving that is philosophy is always the receiving of a whispering—that of the retreating gathering-we—that only the thinker is in a position to hear. It is also the last re-opening of the silence of the world (historical being). It teaches that when the gathering gathers the power to command once again, no one will fail to receive it.

The ego, mine and yours, is the place of dwelling of other egos. Perhaps Socrates was the first example of this awareness and thus the first gatherer.

For Hegel the gathering-we is the 'community of minds'. For the poet, Tasos Livaditis, it is the 'great mystery': 'the beautiful mystery of being alone, the mystery of the two, or the great mystery of the gathering of us all'. The gathering-we is the 'voyage into the open, where nothing is below or above us, and we stand in solitude with ourselves alone'. This aloneness is the universal opening in which the gathering-we unfolds and re-folds as alone. The gathering-we is thus an infinite intensifying in the limitless stillness of its immediacy. It is 'self-moving self-sameness'. The gathering-we is pulsating; it implodes in its formlessness in order to (re)create form out of itself.

The gathering-we is so powerful that it even enables divinities to spring from it without destroying itself. The only place of dwelling for the divine is the gathering of the gathering-we that is more divine than the divine itself. It also destroys the divine without destroying itself since the divine cannot ultimately withstand the power of the gathering. More importantly, the gathering-we does not differentiate between the living and dead, those in the future and those in the present, the human and the non-human. All are particulars that gather in the gathering-we and, as gathered, they are elevated to places of gathering. The whole of humanity can gather under one tree just as it can gather in a single death, that of a Palestinian child for instance. What is infinitely singular—that which is gathered in the gathering—is also the power to expand infinitely and to act as the *topos* of the happening of the gathering. This expansion is the secret of the ego.

How does one 'measure' the scope, or rather, the intensity of the gathering's encompassing of itself? Everything depends on the power that a gathering-we can generate to embrace itself and thereby gather as the gathering. In order to appreciate this claim one must bear in mind that no gathering is unconditionally given, even though throughout history various forms of the gathering may well be presented as givens. There is something more primordial than an already historically realized gathering. That which is more primordial than the gathering is the primordial *as gathering*. In any of its determinate manifestations the world of gathering and the gathering as a world—gatherings are always worlds—respond, implicitly or explicitly, to the power or vision to gather where the vision is itself a form of gathering.

In the philosopher the gathering gives itself the kiss of death.

The smallest gap conceivable between two palms is always greater than the greatest distance possible.

Who is the philosopher? The philosopher is the gatherer mourning the death of the gathering in him.

The primordial gathering of the gathered-to-be—the gathering in and through which the idea of gathering is manifested in visionary terms—is the formless, indeterminate gathering that challenges itself to create form out of its very indeterminacy. To participate in such a project of indeterminate gathering one relies upon two elements of experience. One is the experience of primordial communal being that remains unconditioned by any institutional form and a second is the experience of individual agency as free to receive the command and thus as already in and beyond institutions. The formed gathering-we with the power to refer itself to the simplicity of the formless gathering and thereby perpetually to retrieve it, is the gathering that is flooded with free singularities who perpetually receive the command and thus perpetually address, and are addressed by, the indeterminate gathering. This perpetual receiving through retrieving is what animates the formed world of gathering that manifests a radical sameness in perpetually renewing itself. The life of the gathering is the pulsating movement between the eternal command and its reception, on the one hand, and the historical world of the formed gathering, on the other. The world of such a realized gathering would be a philosophical world in the speculative sense in so far as it is a world whose being directly addresses and embodies the eternal idea of the gathering.

Unlike gatherings that do not address the notion of gathering at all and so are unable to identify the indeterminate gathering as the source of their world, an already realized (determinate) gathering-we can also be philosophical in so far as it renders explicit the visionary notion that it denies. Such a denial presupposes that the appearance of the indeterminate and visionary gathering amidst the historical being of a realized gathering that ultimately denies the vision, renders explicit the project of the thinking/being co-belonging of the gathering-we. Due to the radicality of the vision and its denial, the form of the realized gathering is re-appropriated via the mediation of such denial. Here, it is posited as the form of the being of the gathering-we that empties itself out of its notion and this leads to the corresponding emptying out of the notion itself from its own being, that of the realized gathering. It is the realized gathering that produces an infinite distance from itself in that it denies what mostly belongs to it, namely the very idea of gathering. In this sense the realized gathering-we dwells in the emptiness of its being. This mutual emptying out ultimately refers both being and thought to the denied indeterminate gathering in which and as which the visionary project of the thinking/being co-belonging first becomes an issue philosophically. Philosophy presupposes the denial of the vision by the realized (determinate) gathering and the corresponding retreat of the indeterminate gathering in its own visionary space. Through this retreat thought and being emerge philosophically as infinitely separated.

The real challenge of the philosopher isn't to be a great thinker. The real challenge is to withstand greatness, that of the gathering's retreat. It is there that history floods thinking with the danger of drowning the thinker in the perpetually present.

In so far as the gathering-we challenges the ultimate given, life itself, the gathering constitutes the (di)vision:

anamnesic (the philosophical concept) as amnesic (political being). The awareness incorporated in such (di)vision is the awareness of history. History is the gathering moving towards itself or the gathering that gathers itself. As history, the gathering dwells in the opening of its aloneness and moves towards opening this opening, towards making this opening happen as a perpetual happening. It is the 'wound that heals itself'. It is the 'wound and the knife' but also the wound and the healing. The philosophy of the gathering is the announcement of both this healing and is itself a form of healing.

'Know thyself', 'Love each other', 'Be as a world': where do these three formulations of the command of the indeterminate gathering-we appear, what is their precise meaning and significance, and how are they related to each other? More importantly why does the command appear at all? These commands emerge as irruptions and disruptions through which the indeterminate gathering-we gathers by announcing its idea in visionary terms. They are acts of defiance in and against the plane of dispersion and the corresponding dictatorship of form, that is, of history itself. They are also acts of vision for a renewed encounter between the indeterminate gathering and the formed gathering that will bring about liberation from history through a liberated history. They reject the linear process of history that takes us from one set of forms to another, and in its place they propose the pulsating momentum from indeterminacy to determination and from the determinate to the indeterminate. The real challenge then isn't the creation of the new, but the perpetual and radical renewing of the same, the perpetual birth of what is already born. What is born itself gives birth to what will give birth to it. The indeterminate gathering is always the new because it is perpetually the oldest, and it is the oldest because it is older than time itself. The oldest though always comes last as the first by annihilating time.

It is only love that makes one property-less, that is, being-less.

What is dispersion? It is the mode of being of the indeterminate gathering when its indeterminacy is invisible to it. The indeterminate holds; dispersion separates. Dispersion is the indeterminate as blind. There is a moment in history that reveals history itself as the falling apart of the indeterminate and the determinate. Between them there is the abyss of violence of the objective order and the violence of the abyss of the subjective emptiness of the ego in a perpetual exchange. The indeterminate emerges as dispersion- the set of subjectivities trapped in their internal spaces without possibility of escaping, which is an infinite escaping. It is the visionless indeterminate gathering of atomic, and thus blind, egos that unfolds by perpetually sinking in its own amnesia as amnesic. As sinking it releases the order of form that history is upon which it absolutely depends as dependent, since it is claimed by this order not as freely embracing its claiming but as the infinitely powerless finite. The power of form and the powerlessness of the gathering of dispersion go together. The net result is that the power of form isn't powerful enough to also act as the destroyer of its world by recognizing the indeterminate gathering-we as the creator of determination and itself as the creator of indeterminacy. On the other hand as dispersion, the indeterminate gathering of atomic egos is infinitely powerless, and thus powerful in its inability to project the vision of form, or in its ability to sink in its amnesia. Any vision of the gathering is thus a disturbance of dispersion and of amnesic form and a radical reformulation of indeterminacy as the bearer of the notion of the gathering to come- the gathering that infinitely gathers, that is, determines itself as a world.

The empty self is the self not possessed by the communal body.

The solidarity of the gathered and the aloneness of the gatherer.

The formed world of the gathering of the dispersion of egos expresses the moment of the self-othering of the gathering-we. It is the gathering producing and surrounding itself by the parts of the dismembering of its visionary body. Out of the dispersing egos the dispersion of dispersion arises as the dispersion of forms of dispersion and as the dispersion of the ego itself. It is the negative moment of the negation of the very idea and practice of gathering, and thus an infinite negation, death itself. At the same time, what is negated occasionally emerges as the vision of the life of the gathering in order to announce the immanent relation of dispersion with the indeterminate gathering as what mostly belongs to it. The hidden vision of history is to transform dispersion into visionary, all encompassing indeterminacy. Whenever it becomes momentarily explicit, such a vision functions as the magnifying glass that enlarges the unfolding of the death of the gathering. It does so by presenting the gathering as the ultimate source of love, thus allowing the philosopher to see by becoming a seer. Thinking is the magnification of the infinite—the intensification of the infinite—the always achieved through the intensification of the finitude of the thinker as the practice of thinking. Differently put, philosophy is the vision the gathering has of itself whilst in a state of death. Not even life is a given for the gathering and for philosophy. In formulating the vision of love of the gathering, the philosopher dies the death of the gathering on the plane of history, which is this death and this dying.

On the plane of history, that of the unfolding of dispersion and the corresponding arrogance of form, the seer of love walks amongst dismembered bodies.

Hegel and Nietzsche have their common root in Plato, the first modern. Plato is the first modern because he is the first seer. His thinking developed through the radical experience of the activation of the event of dispersion that still shapes the world today. His thought captures the moment where the dispersion of atomic egos, or, according to Hegel, private persons, emerges violently as an infinite force of corruption, by destroying the

Greek gathering. As destroyed the gathering becomes reflective in Plato's philosophy in and through which it seeks its principle. Because the gathering *as such* thus becomes an issue, the indeterminate gathering also takes central stage for the first time. The event of the indeterminate gathering had already appeared in the philosophical practice of Socrates and his friends. Socrates asks the Athenian gathering to recreate itself out of the indeterminate gathering of the friends of the philosopher around the philosopher who brings to all the dark command, 'know thyself'. The seeking of form that the command commands presupposes the dismantling of the given forms of the *polis* and the new profound experience of the indeterminate gathering. For Plato, the ultimate source of the seeking of forms is the experience of the indeterminate gathering as the perpetual and primordial urge of the gathering to gather itself. Plato's encounter with the force of the plane of dispersion of the emerging atomic egos was so dramatically intense, he realized that as a member of the gathering of dispersion the ego is also itself a field of dispersion.

It is the simple that can accommodate complexity as celebration or mourning.

The world of the gathering expects us. The world is as expecting.

Depth is horizontal.

Transparency is a creative illusion.

After Hegel we have a shift from the moment of philosophy to the philosophies of the moment.

We can think, or rather must think, Plato and Hegel, as the two parentheses or as the two palms, of an embracing that delimits the space of the opening and the closing of history *as history*. One unfolds at the moment of the explosion of the dispersing, and formulates the vision of what is left behind by such explosion. The other unfolds at the moment of the activation of the implosion of the dispersing and its world, and formulates the arriving vision of the gathering-we. One begins with the already defeated notion of the gathering-we as eternally defeated, and seeks its being not in the notion itself but in the realm of human finitude. The other begins with the defeated being of the revolution of the gathering-we, and seeks the notion of the gathering and its realization in terms that incorporate history. As articulated in *The Republic*, Plato's gathering is the very idea of the gathering that gathers itself as left behind by the dispersing, as what is left behind, the gathering never to be realized. On the other hand, Hegel's gathering is what leaves the dispersing behind by thinking it, that is, by incorporating it into itself as its world evolving towards a final prolonged collapse that will release the indeterminate gathering. In both cases history is experienced as the realm of being that is emptied of its notion or, in other words, as time that is emptied of eternity.

With Plato the emptiness of empty time is unfulfilled. The world of dispersion that emerges historically with the Romans turns against its fundamental principles in order to re-appropriate them through Christianity in an ultimate act of the victorious form expressed by the modern state. Form is destroyed and its dominance over the gathering of dispersion is replaced by the infinite will of the individual, the emperor. With Hegel empty time has been fulfilled and the world becomes the realm of triumphant narcissism, the perpetual present, the ultimate triumph of form, or of history. Between the two we have the rise and the fall of Christianity. Christianity is the most faithful servant of form. It is the Judas that betrays the indeterminate gathering of Christ and his followers to the church and the state. At the same time, however, it is the only real opponent of the speculative in so far as it sets the challenge and it posits itself as the only satisfactory response: transforming the insignificant singularity of the ego into significant agency via the love of God.

History unfolds on the plane of ownership.

The phenomenon of the dispersion of atomic egos becomes fully explicit on the plane of its own unfolding, when its principle becomes available. By negating the future it makes the future empty, an emptiness that is then filled by the immersion of the empty self in the emptiness it has created. This is the command: 'be as a person and respect others as persons'. This command is ultimate, but ultimate only in principle. Therefore it isn't the command of the ultimate, as liberals think. This is the great command, not of the circularity of the ego's embrace of the gathering but of the linearity of infinite distance between egos, which are flashing points in the horizon of dispersion. The infinite distance between empty egos can be travelled only by the command 'be as a person'. Not the cosmic aloneness of the gathering-we but the loneliness of the dispersed 'I'. Atomic egos flash as they emerge, and they emerge as owners of 'things'. The ego is the flashing in the thing owned. The ontology (manifestation) and the ethics (recognition) of private property here acquire central historical stage by being elevated to the force of history, the ultimate ground of narcissistic and thus violent form.

With elemental simplicity, Hegel's historical vision reveals what is elemental in the shapes that the world of the gathering-we takes as it moves on the plane of history as this history. According to this vision the period beginning with the demise of the Greek world and the rise of the Roman—a period extending to the current era of the developing global order—marks the emergence and slow unfolding of one and the same phenomenon, that of the actuality of the formal subject. We might read this entire epoch in terms of the taking place of the gathering as the dispersing of formal subjects that infinitely repel each other as repelling and as repelled, while at the same time recognizing each other as having the infinite right of repelling and the infinite duty to accept themselves as repelled. Property ownership is at the centre here, and the aim is the radicalization of property-owning subjectivity. 'I am by excluding from what I own the whole set of other property owners that is boundless in number and dispersed in the infinity of space.' At the same time, institutions spring from and as this exclusion.

In liberal modernity forms no longer succeed each other in an unceasing process of emerging and disappearing; they stand next to each other as dispersed from each other whilst they themselves are forms of dispersion. The dictatorship of forms is also a dictatorship over forms. By the time history fully emerges, time is subordinated to the 'space' marking the co-existence of forms. That a form is a particular isn't demonstrated through its demise and the appearance of another form. Particularity is already its mode of being since other forms already surround it on the plane of an already established differentiation. Modernity's differentiation reduces time to the act of recognition of what is already the case. Time is subordinated to the principle of the formal universality of particularity, which realizes itself with infinite speed across the plane of history. The logic of the formal universality of particularity is given by what Hegel calls the disjunctive syllogism: 'A is either B or C or D. But A is neither C nor D. Therefore A is B'.

Not Socrates but Plato. The one who died for philosophy was Socrates but the one who died philosophically was Plato. That is why Plato is the first philosopher.

Any encounter with genuine thinkers is always a deferral that takes the form of a promise for, and anticipation of, what will become a more radical and revealing engagement in some future reading. The practice of revisiting the intellectual landscapes of our fellow thinkers would not eventuate but for the recognition of the essentially preliminary and preparatory nature of previous visits.

Death is the site of gathering for the living. In the collective ethos of those who respond to any form of the command 'be as a world' sacrifice becomes the ultimate realization of the subject as a place of dwelling and of others' gathering. In these circumstances even one's absolute absence is significant as a place of gathering. It is no accident that the three commands are directly associated with sacrifice (Socrates, Christ, French Revolution).

Capitalism is the ground on which the Christian and the speculative struggle for supremacy—the affirmation of uniqueness, transforming the contingent into significant, without destroying contingency.

The revolution was the irruption in and the disruption of the flow of history through and as the emergence of the amorphous and visionary gathering of visionary minds. If history is the order of being, the gathering's determinate differentiation into 'masses' or 'spheres', the revolution interrupted history as the 'negativity' that 'permeated all its moments'. The result was that 'all social groups or classes which are the spiritual into which the whole is articulated are abolished.' What appeared for the first time through such radical negation and as this very negation was the simplicity of the whole, the 'undivided Substance of absolute freedom'. It is precisely because freedom was experienced as immanently related to the objectivity of communal substance holding finite wills together in its silence that it was also experienced as absolute. It was the freedom of the singular will that was at once infinitely permeated, and thus unconditionally claimed by the infinite power of the communal bond of the indeterminate gathering, whilst being released through such claiming as what could infinitely expand and embrace this bond. The communality of the indeterminate gathering was what Hegel referred to as the 'object as notion', the universal as the *topos* of dwelling of particulars encountering each other as already gathered. And in being released by the universal in order to embrace the universal, gathered wills were called upon to think the universal as the gathering of the gathered. In other words they were called to act as visionaries that could provide the being and the very idea of the communal gathering. 'Never since the sun had stood in the firmament and the planets revolved around him had it been perceived that man's existence centred in his head, i.e. in Thought, inspired by which he builds up the world of reality'.

The indeterminate gathering gathers singular visions of the gathering to come. The indeterminate gathering gathers gatherers.

The revolution was the irruption of the amorphous gathering of wills that, by incorporating both, was at once beyond time (the order of being), and eternity (the notion). As this act of pure manifestation that seeks its own manifesting, the gathering posits the idea of the philosophical world. The indeterminate communal gathering posed the challenge of creating the form and being of the gathering as such out of the abyss of its formlessness.

If for the revolution it was true that we are already in the gathering as gathered then the fundamental question for us isn't one of identity but one of dwelling. Not 'who are we?' but 'where do we come from and where are we going?'. In a flash the revolution provided an unconditional answer: we come from the gathering and we are moving towards the gathering. It is as this movement that the gathering gathers itself and produces form out of its formlessness. What is history then if not the drowning of the formless in the formed, the inability of the order of being to acknowledge the power of the gathering to create order and also negate it? This is why the first act of the revolution was to destroy history, the differentiation that was unable to refer itself to its own source, in order for the eternal and time to emerge in the emerging of the gathering.

The fate of the individual is the gathering.

Hegel's philosophy was experienced as (the articulation of the idea of) dwelling in the revolutionary *topos* of the gathering-we. For the first time after Plato, philosophy could claim the gathering of revolutionary wills as its *topos* and thus treat all other philosophy as dwelling in the prison cell of formal thinking, which always needs a proposition to activate itself without ever knowing where the proposition comes from. Since Hegel, the reactivation of philosophy must involve a returning to itself from its own *topos*. It is the light of the galaxy in the cosmic darkness of the abyss that our communal fate is, and must be measured by the darkness it can carry.

What the philosopher hears is the last call of the call—the call whispering. But the whisper is louder than the call because in whispering the call has as its horizon its already posited silence.

The revolution was the event that reactivated time by revealing eternity, the only gathering thus far that brought together being and justice in a single vision (Yeats). Being the child of eternity, philosophy can only happen in the *topos* that the revolution is and can only be the *topos* where the revolutionary gathering gathers. Is there any doubt that this is the lesson of Plato, the first philosopher of the revolution in all the senses of the word 'first'? He emerges in the revolutionary gathering of Socrates and his friends in order ultimately and through a torturous process to offer in his *Republic* the place for this gathering to gather. The truly accomplished philosopher can be either the first or the last. In between there is only thinking, wondering around in the prison cell of its formal structures unable to be informed by its *topos* of dwelling. Aristotle was the initial philosopher occupying the space of the in-between. He substituted wonder for the philosopher's terror of being rejected by the gathering of the city as the *topos* of the thinker's dwelling. Hegel was the last philosopher. His thinking was that of the French Revolution, the last revolution after the Socratic first. What is decisive about this particular (a) historical event that activates (an already activated) history and (an already activated) philosophy? Through it we enter the realms of history *as such*, and of pure philosophy, because it brings on the scene the idea and the challenge of creating the world as philosophical. The need for philosophy can be felt and philosophy can be activated only in a world that is philosophical. Dwelling in such a world is the supreme presupposition of philosophical thinking. This is a speculative proposition that forms the conceptual core of Hegel's thought and the fundamental experience of the Hegelian philosopher.

Only a philosophical world can be the bearer of the idea of pure liberation, but also the practice of pure terror.

The first act of thinking is the uttering of the 'we' and the 'we' is the first thought.

Owning is thinking emptily.

For the thinker the task today, and always, is neither to mourn over the dead communal body nor to try to resurrect it. The task is rather to enter its death, to make its death one's own. If this is indeed possible then in the dying of the thinker the death of the communal body itself dies and thus love is liberated in the vision that philosophy is. Those who refuse to die are condemned not to love.

The thinker unreservedly receives the call to die, and he is this receiving.

Philosophies of the event are usually an attempt to discipline the event.

After the French Revolution there can be no revolution.

Being is the justice of thinking and thinking the justice of being.

The communal gathering of singularities releases the singular as gathered by positing it as the bearer of its idea, the vision of differentiation as the gathering of the gathering. What draws the singular infinitely into the substantive bond is its release from it. Claiming is releasing, and releasing is the vision of thinking, that is, differentiation. This is the vision of truth or justice, the idea of the mutual informing of the being with the notion of the gathering. The source both of being and thinking is the indeterminate gathering in the abyss of its non-specificity. The indeterminate gathering of wills is the gathering of visions of the gathering.

The indeterminate gathering of pure wills is what holds being and justice in a single vision. It is that which makes the issue of the interrelation of the being of the gathering (time) and the notion of the gathering (eternal) a project.

The revolution announced (content); it did not practice (form).

Thinkers today fail to admit that the world terrorizes them in a way that it didn't for Hegel and Marx. Thinkers today are lions without teeth, eagles without wings.

Intensification is a falling back into what one attempts to overcome precisely because one attempts to overcome it.

Concepts are created. They also demand to be received. But only the eternal can be received.

History is the power that destroys formed gatherings, not in order to replace them with another form in a perpetual and meaningless becoming that Nietzsche detested so much, but in order to reveal the 'absolute freedom' of the indeterminate gathering-we as the universal power that is a 'maker and shaper' of form. This is the 'achieved community of minds' whose members, precisely because they are 'minds', are both singular and, as thinking, infinitely expanding to embrace the gathering by providing its very idea. They are at once as gathered and as receiving the command that the indeterminate gathering-we is to gather the gathering by being 'a reciprocity of self-consciousness in the form of universality and of a personal consciousness'. Responding to this command means exploring the possibilities and the significance of creating form out of this state of indeterminacy in such a way that the created form (historical) has the power perpetually to recognize the indeterminate gathering (non-historical) as the source of creativity by perpetually dissolving itself in order to repeat itself. Dwelling in the gathering is a philosophical dwelling. For Hegel then radical politics (and philosophy) is the activation and development of the genealogy of the whole as the gathered gathering in the thinking and acting of single minds that recognize (embrace) each other as embracing the whole. His theory of the syllogism was designed to capture this pulsating movement from the indeterminate to the determinate and from the determinate to the indeterminate.

Liberalism: the voiceless era of the many voices; freedom without integrity.

The tragedy of twentieth century thought: we have yet to enter the nineteenth century.

The vision of philosophy is less in what it says and more in what it does.

With the French Revolution the indeterminate gathering-we and the associated vision of the expanding self and the gathering that gathers itself emerged out of history as the non-historical. In the failure of the Revolution they retreated back and took the form of the pure vision of what is coming. Speculative philosophy is directly related to the retreat of the indeterminate gathering-we. It captures the fact that in the event of the Revolution something fundamental was announced and tries to uncover the meaning of this announcement. The philosophical self is thus released in the beyond and expands as thinking in order to embrace in a visionary manner the vision of the world of the gathering-we.

In the history of the West, activated by the French Revolution and its command, 'be as a world', the indeterminate gathering-we was the third instance of the unfolding of the relation between history and the non-historical. The first was announced by the ancient Greek command, 'know thyself', which was politically introduced by the indeterminate gathering of the friends of the philosopher around Socrates who called upon the Athenians to recreate the city by listening to the command. This found its philosophical expression in Plato's *Republic* where the aim of the exercise is to create the formed gathering of the 'Kallipolis' out of the indeterminate gathering of Socrates and his comrades. The second instance was the indeterminate gathering of the Christians, which formed around the command, 'love each other'. Speculative philosophy was the direct outcome of the third instance of the appearance of the indeterminate gathering associated with the event of 1789.

Hegel is the philosopher who philosophizes without philosophers. His antipodes is Derrida.

Hegel answers. Heidegger asks.

What is the task of philosophy? To think concepts without concepts.

Philosophy is an embracing of what embraces, an accepting.

The revolution released the vision of unconditional creativity or absolute freedom not through the painstaking and systematic deconstruction of texts of any kind but through the apocalyptic destruction of the whole historical landscape. It was the 'sunburst which, in one flash, illuminates the features of the new world' and itself as this power of illuminating. The deconstruction of philosophy that speculative philosophy (history of philosophy) enacted presupposes the radical all-encompassing practice of scepticism as practiced by the event of the revolution, and philosophy is the practicing of the idea of such scepticism as a precondition for the philosophical enactment of the world. It is no accident then that Hegel relates philosophy to the 'resolve of the will to think purely' as 'the freedom that abstracts from everything, and grasps its own abstraction, the simplicity of thinking'. Such a resolve is activated by a certain kind of dwelling in the spaces of freedom opened by the release of the indeterminate gathering. It follows that the challenge for philosophy isn't to present itself as the destroyer of the monopoly of form in history, but to appreciate history as the destroyer of everything particular—including the given conceptual forms of philosophy—as well as itself as this destroyer. History *as such* is revealed not in the act of replacing one set of forms with another—actually this process hides history—but in the ultimate act of negating the realm of forms and negating its negation as what will give rise to another similarly historical realm. History effaces itself as the bad infinite of the becoming of becoming with the liberation of the indeterminate gathering-we through this double negating.

The world is already opened to the thinking of radical philosophy because, as the absolute destroyer of the givenness of the order associated with its structures, it is already philosophical, that is, unconditionally free, self-manifesting. It is philosophical though, not because it can be thought through the application of already given conceptual schemes, but because the world of the gathering-we itself activates thinking through which its very idea is enacted. As self-manifesting the gathering-we contains both the being and the thinking of manifestation.

RHAPSODIES OF EMPTINESS
(NOTES FOR A BOOK OF THE FUTURE)

I

Unlike Derrida Hegel doesn't need actual texts to appreciate the conceptual moment they articulate because appreciating such a moment is the precondition for making sense of the significance of texts. So, for example, if none of Plato's writings were available to us we could still make sense of the Platonic moment in thought as a necessary aspect of world history. Of course the same is true for history as a whole. From a speculative perspective we don't need empirical data to appreciate the stages of the development of the gathering-we. We presuppose such an appreciation in order to meaningfully situate empirical data. Here however we don't refer to some kind of a-priori approach that grounds itself on the given structures of some kind of world mind. Rather we refer to history as the succession of different gatherings of forms of gathering activated by the power to gather immanently to the gathering. What is a priori is the intensity of significance, not the form. The aim of history is to posit the gathering as what gathers itself, as the self-gathered and thus as what makes itself into a project through the relational dynamics of the determinate and the indeterminate gathering. Once history releases the indeterminate gathering from within it, the meaning of history is activated as part of the gathering's vision to gather itself. Therefore the idea of history can be captured and history can be made to happen (philosophically) as history from within its own ungrounded ground. It follows from this that only by appreciating history as the unfolding of significance, and more specifically the form of history that ultimately gives rise to the indeterminate gathering, will we be able to identify the historical opening in which philosophy after Hegel, and specifically its more significant Nietzschean moment, emerges.

2

As the gathering that gathers itself, history releases the indeterminate gathering-we as the gathering that announces itself as a project when it has reached the stage that succeeds and cancels the historical. This is the stage of history as the dispersion of forms in which particular forms are, by recognizing their historicity as absolute, that is, in terms that takes them beyond time. How is this possible? If history is the realm of forms (of the gathering), which, individually and collectively, fail to recognize the moment of freedom—the creative moment of the relation between indeterminacy and determination—such a realm acquires its state when the order of forms absorbs the indeterminate gathering into its order. For this order of forms nothing is beyond since the only thing that can occupy this beyond, namely the non-historical, is already incorporated into and disciplined by its structures. This 'blindness' is the intensity of dispersion.

Here the indeterminate gathering is treated not as the creator of form but as that which has the potential to undermine the given world of form. To perpetually counteract this negating tendency is a matter of the realm of form intensifying itself, not by opening itself to the creative act of eternally enacting the determinate gathering-we through the affirmation of radical indeterminacy, but by disciplining the indeterminate gathering. The realm of form doesn't create itself by emerging out of indeterminacy; it perpetuates itself by expanding the horizontality of a dispersing dispersion. Forms are historical, not because other forms transcend them in time, but because they co-exist with other forms in a world of unlimitedly expanding pluralism. When historical time is transformed into the time of history it becomes the slave of space. Time can no longer offer us the possibility of salvation. The verdict 'there is no future' is axiomatic and final.

3

As disciplined, the indeterminate gathering is abstract. It emerges in its lifeless principle as an announcement and thus as a desire or as a prophet. It is the indeterminate gathering empty of its power, one that ultimately gravitates, not towards the creation, but towards the disintegration of form. This is the gathering of persons as exclusively monadic, supremely unable to receive the command to gather and so to transform themselves into bearers of the idea and the world of the gathering. These are the empty selves, orphans of the inner, consumed by the *pathos* for the outer, perpetually emptying themselves out of the (speculative) power to expand (to think). They achieve this emptying out by relating to the world of form as an infinite authority that, silently and without commanding, affirms its world as the only world. Here we have a double emptiness: the world is empty of the indeterminate gathering, the indeterminate gathering empty of world. It is history as this emptiness that implodes and occasionally releases the creative power that the indeterminate gathering-we is, by liberating the monadic self's singularity from exclusively being a secret, a whisper dispersed on the plane of dispersion.

4

The monadic person is an unlimited limitation since the limitation to its atomicity is this atomicity itself. Its singularity isn't experienced as what also releases the maddening and disorienting intensity of the expanding self that embraces the gathering-we. It is rather experienced as the mystery of an implosion, the impossible implosion of the singular that excludes the possibility of anything dwelling in it. It is thus the inner in a finite manner, the inner that like a dragon guards its innerness. Here finitude is affirmed as the empty space of emptiness that guards its boundaries by not allowing the other to dwell in it. The monadic self is the infinite non-encountering of the other outside of itself, by being this outside itself. But the self that abandons itself by moving into the sphere of the purely outer, thus becoming a ghost, encounters the owner of the thing as the outer of the other self. It emerges in the world from its secret innerness as the supremely non-exclusive owner of external things. Not the gathering, but the soulless thing as owned is what mediates the encounter of soulless selves.

As property owners, selves are dispersed from each other and in themselves become the plane of dispersion of desires, aims, dreams. More importantly, being themselves monadic, owners are infinitely non-satisfiable at the very core of their singularity. Owners are, by being eternally yearning, that is, by moving around in the emptiness of their moving around on planes populated by the empty presence of things and the equally empty absence of selves. Owners are monadic and nomadic. It is this scattering of the inner and this dispersion of the outer that is disciplined by the order of forms through its legal, economic, and political institutions agonising not for integration but for containing an already achieved disintegration.

5

The immediate, that is immemorial or proud 'impenetrability' flooding the inner of the monadic self, is in fact mediated. This is where the drama starts. It is mediated by the emptying out of what mostly belongs to the self and its world, namely the eroticism of the speculative and the corresponding speculative vision of the world. Such emptying out occurs when the self encounters the other self via the acknowledging involved in ownership and exchange of things determined, not by the implosion of embracing that makes the many one, but the explosion of exclusion that makes the one many. So not only is the self-empty; its emptiness is also empty since the self is unaware of the speculative as the emptied out. The saddest thing is an empty emptiness, like an office employee taking lunch in the park alone. The awareness of the monadic self is a forgetting, not of being, but of loving. On the other hand, the awareness of mediation belongs only to the speculative thinker who dies and is willing to die the death of love. The speculative thinker lives in the tension created by the forgetfulness of the outer and the loving of the inner. But since, in the global spaces of owning and exchange, the self is the emptying out unable to relate to the speculative as the emptied out, it acts as the emptying out by turning itself towards the only thing available to it, namely its emptiness. Because the fundamental experience of the self is its mediated immediacy as this forgetting, ultimately the self relates to itself as the empty aim of emptying of its emptiness. Consequently, the empty self registers the element of mediation as the empty urge to empty itself of its emptiness. What form does this urge take? Given this urge, and as this urge, the self extends itself towards the speculative—it seeks the speculative from a distance, the infinite distance of its emptiness—and against its emptiness and the world of emptiness. It is, by somehow capturing glimpses of the mirage of the speculative. At the same time, because in doing so, it affirms its emptiness, and thus its forgetting, it falls back into it by turning against the speculative, which, from the same distance that it seeks it, now seems an infinitely oppressive force, the source of a new slavery. This means that the empty self creates a vision of the beyond of itself and its world filled with speculative elements in abstraction from what makes the speculative, speculative, namely the notion and the practice of the erotic thinking of the dead gatherer. Therefore, the speculative vision of the pulsating love of the gathering is violently metamorphosed into the thirst for a life preserved in the circle of time, a return of the same not an arriving of the arrived. But love doesn't return because it never turns. It is here that we have the discovery of nihilism. More precisely, the (non) thinking of the monadic self fails to recognise and affirm the justice that the concept demands, the direct relation of the conceptual forms produced by speculative thinking with the fundamental experience of the innerness of the indeterminate gathering-we that never moves. For the bond of love is substituted by the dispersion of life. Happiness floods the plane of history as the true meaning of history, as its accomplished *telos*. The time of the Nietzschean gathering has arrived because the appropriate place has been opened.

6

The moment of the place must occur for the Nietzschean gathering to gather. Nietzsche's unsurpassed and unsurpassable historical role was to make this happen as a happening that happens in this making. He enacted the Nietzschean moment and became the single founding member of the corresponding gathering as its gatherer. Nietzsche demonstrated that in order for the thinker to think, thinking must be activated through the enactment of the moment itself. But what does this enactment involve? In so far as the empty self is determined by its tendency towards the speculative, it becomes imperative to encounter the dynamics of the indeterminate gathering as the beyond of history in which history collapses. As this beyond the indeterminate functions as the place in which thinking can occur as a thinking liberated from the regimes of form and order, a thinking without concepts and as the justice of concepts. At the same time, given that, unlike the speculatively expanding self, the empty self doesn't emerge as merging—as the loved loving—through the event of the indeterminate gathering-we, it posits itself as the space of the happening of such gathering. This follows from the fact that the empty self is already a participant in the dispersal of monadic selves. Due to its given situatedness in the field of dispersion that is already disciplined by the order of history the seeking of the speculative expresses the desire of the dispersed self to enact the indeterminate gathering that is emancipated from this order. This is what Zarathustra attempts to achieve by becoming the *topos* in which his friends gather. At the same time, due to its emptiness the seeking of the empty self is itself empty. This is why the justification offered for Zarathustra's descent, for his going 'under', is an abstract one; it directly relates to the fact that Zarathustra's seeking isn't grounded in what he seeks. It isn't the indeterminate gathering that unconditionally commands the self, which is already gathered by the gathering, to enact the gathering; rather it is the emptiness of the self that drives the self towards enacting, and thus grounding, the indeterminate gathering. As this desire, the empty self posits itself as the place where the dispersal of monadic selves can be transformed into the indeterminate gathering, thus liberating the non-historical from history. But here the indeterminate gathering, and the corresponding vision of the world as visionary, isn't encountered as what actually happens through the implosion of history itself but as an aim to be announced and realized by the exceptional individual who appears from within the landscape of history and posits itself as pointing to the beyond. This pointing is of course visionary. However, the vision isn't the world itself as this vision (history as the inner drive towards the indeterminate gathering-we) but the vision that the thinker brings to the world. Consequently it isn't the thinker who stands in the, in principle, complete world as the opening in which thinking is to take place. Rather, it is the overman 'in whom the world stands complete'. Unlike the speculative thinker who comes late because the world as a whole has already exhausted itself in the narcissism of the 'happy' outer, a happening that transforms the whole into a vision conceptualized by philosophy, the empty self comes early, or untimely, and brings the vision to the world which is empty of vision. But such untimely vision is empty of world precisely because it cannot think of itself as the vision that already belongs to the world. There is no way for the thinker to bridge the abyss between himself and the world as the bearer of the vision, because, in spite of its speculative character, such a vision is formal, loveless. It thinks of history, and the speculative, not as what liberates itself from its own order but as what is trapped in such order. The thinker then is the suspended speculative. The thinker captures the core of the speculative but without the 'heart' that makes it loving, the world, history, and the indeterminate gathering-we. Consequently, Nietzsche's vision remains empty. The idea of the eternal return of the same is equally profound and empty. Nietzsche announces the idea as a poet and abandons it as a philosopher. Nietzsche is the thinker suspended between life and death.

7

But if we exclude history from revealing the beyond of history, if we become deaf to the indeterminate gathering that bears the thinker as the thinker of the gathering, who is the bearer of the bearer of the vision? It is only the empty self that performs the double role of its emptiness. Consequently, it is the empty self as the thinker that has the vision of the one who brings the vision. This is Nietzsche performing the role of Zarathustra. As the bearer of the vision Zarathustra posits himself as the place where his students gather in order for him to announce the overman and the eternal return of the same. It is the vision that the thinker has of himself as the bearer of the vision and the corresponding announcement that replaces the revolution as the agent who announces to the thinker the idea of the eternal return of the same and commands him to think (in) it. Without the revolution and its retreat the thinker emerges as a head dispersed into its many eyes.

8

What Nietzsche offers is profound enough to make it possible for the vision of the beyond of this world to emerge. However, what emerges is so abstract—the mere shadow of a vision—that it sinks into its abstractness. And it is in this sinking that what really emerges is the already emerged, namely the concrete world *as such* with all the majestic terror of the one and only world. In its turn, this full exposure of the world as the only available world, itself intensifies the yearning for the beyond since it transforms it into the empty yearning of those unable to overcome and thus incapable of reconciling themselves with reality. No matter what the philosopher says, in his prophesies he never gains the company of those who come from outside history. He remains surrounded and haunted by dead and dismembered bodies that populate history. The philosopher turns himself into the place of dwelling of the dead ones. In his attempt to overcome the world of order by going 'under' he becomes the underworld and his saying is not the place of truth but the sermon of a supreme *thanatology*—his own.

9

The beyond of history, which Nietzsche attempted to open in order to situate himself, is beyond itself and therefore already situated in and thus overpowered by history. History is the beyond of its own beyond, the power that domesticates the desire for this beyond by motivating and, at the same time, annihilating its radical aspirations. It is this nothingness of the beyond that is repeatedly enacted by the Nietzschean gathering. Like the Christian gathering before them, the members of the Nietzschean moment are in the service of a history that exhibits closure precisely because it permits a kind of longing of the beyond in the shape of a prophesy that lives and dies with the prophet. The closure of history and the corresponding totalitarian gesture of the speculative become an issue only through and in the thinking of those who immerse themselves in the world they long to deny by denying it. In the spaces of the Nietzschean gathering thinking is performed as a refusal to expand; affirmation without death.

10

The Nietzschean moment in philosophy is the intensification of the emptiness of the empty self, the abstract longing for the profound that is missing from its core but unable to be given the flesh and bones of a world in which to dwell. Neither a spirit nor a temple, the meaning of the Nietzschean moment is this 'neither'. But it is neither because, in a sense, it is both. It is a spirit without a temple and thus a formless spirit spread everywhere like a dispersed cloud or a desert storm. And it is a temple without a spirit and thus a yet to be enacted temple, the void longing of the void.

11

Perhaps Nietzsche is the first thinker to release shapeless clouds into the distant horizons of visionary thinking. Following him, others, like Heidegger, Derrida, Levinas and Deleuze, dwelt in different corners of the same space. They comprise the Nietzschean gathering of the empty selves desperately trying to empty their emptiness like one who desires to empty the sea. They all looked at the world with empty eyes. But when we look at the world with empty eyes the world looks back at us emptily with the eyes of a skull. In the abyss of such a look we only see the abyss.

Concepts are forms of gathering.

No matter what we think, thinking is gathering.

In leaping one doesn't move and in moving one doesn't leap.

The question of the meaning of being presupposes the experience of the being of meaning.

'The philosopher today finds him or herself tragically caught in a shadow cast from the future, caught between the existing empirical world and the speculative beyond of absolute knowledge' (Paul Ashton).

Don't believe the poets; the time of language has past.

It is only when desire becomes vast enough to crush you that you realize it isn't yours. This is when thinking begins.

The question isn't really 'to be or not to be'. The real question is 'to not-be or to be-not-be'.

From the beginning, Nietzsche's attack of Christianity was a family feud.

Just as vapour rises from the earth, speculative thinking rises from the pores of the poet's skin. This is what both Nietzsche and Kierkegaard knew nothing about.

Two philosophical moments, the Platonic and the Hegelian. The first captures what history left behind, the second, what is to come. Both belong to the surge of the world-forming power of the empty self. Is it an accident that Plato's most philosophical work, *The Republic*, is about justice, and Hegel's most dramatic moment is his *Philosophy of Right*?

The contingent perishes, the unique dies.

Metaphysics wasn't a conceptual telescope; it was the path of rebellion.

The living perishes. The loving dies. Egos die from love and they perish from life. Therefore the mortal perishes and the immortal dies. We become loving by defying life because life is always that of the contingent (natural) whereas love is that of the singular (spiritual).

The indeterminate gathering is the absolute sceptic.

Substantive universal: it is powerful enough to penetrate the impenetrable, but also powerless since it doesn't compromise the uniqueness of the unique.

Formal universal: it is powerless to penetrate the unique, but powerful to transform it into the impersonal. Through this transformation the unique is reduced to the contingent. Only the unique can protect its uniqueness by deconstructing the world of the formal universal.

Transcend the anxiety of perishing in order to enjoy the affirmation of dying.

Our century cannot be that of Hegel because we have yet to retrieve the first book of history, Plato's *Republic*.

Nothing can resist our aloneness.

Plato is the starting point because we've already started.

The time of defeat and the defeat of time come together. This is speculative philosophy.

The gathering is the un-gatherable that gathers. It is the erotic power that both immobilizes and mobilizes agency. As the messenger of the erotic community to come, the philosopher is the loved one who loves. The one who is loved is mad; the one who loves is composed. As the loved one, the self 'feels' itself evaporating. The one who loves has himself gathered in the strange place of the gatherer. Therefore, he is the one who, as Rousseau would say, loves with love. He also announces that for the gathering defeat is impossible. However, this announcement takes place from the immemorial depths of defeat itself. In order for the gathering to emerge, not undefeated, but undefeatable, it must first defeat itself and show the nullity of such defeat. But in order to have integrity, such defeat must be the first and the last. It is here that all the tragedies of the human adventure are located.

The real challenge for philosophy is, not the beginning but 'the beginning before the beginning' (Paul Ashton). And of course this is the challenge of non-beginning.

The fulfilment of time, the time of time, is evil.

The world is a flat plane that implodes into the depth of the past and explodes into the heights of the future.

Perhaps in philosophy the importance of fundamental, world-shaping ideas, has little to do with whether they are 'correct' or 'incorrect'. For the thinker to 'put ideas to the test' is always of secondary importance. Who is capable of attempting this, why, and from where? Fundamental orientations aren't challenged through questioning; they are replaced by another, perhaps more radical, orientation, just as the Christian church replaced the Greek temple, or as the icon replaced the idol. Perhaps, through their uncompromising 'aura' of that which appears as both familiar and strange, always untimely but in the most timely fashion, always other worldly and simultaneously of this world, it is ideas that annihilate collective and personal biographies and put us to the test by calling upon us to present ourselves, (as if in an act of re-birth), as worthy of being called upon. Isn't this the time of revolutions with the one and single aim to end time? Ideas claim, not the rigid and evanescent present, but a perpetual presencing of singularities that experience themselves as simultaneously insignificant and significant. If this is the case, then unlike mathematics, which, as Kant said, carries its apodicticity within itself and therefore demands an impersonal, and impersonally transmissible (democratic) thinking, fundamental ideas carry in their emerging the power of attributing eternal significance to erotic, and therefore communal, singularities. Not to prove, but to emerge in their emerging and thus to think or act through one's singularity is thus the challenge for the thinker who rebels and for the rebel who thinks.

Dead spirit is flat space. It is there that the rhizome flourishes.

The poet proclaims: 'we have many selves, but only one darkness' (Borges). Our darkness is the retreat of the indeterminate gathering.

We have many lives, but only one death. Are philosophers afraid to practice death? Are they afraid to acknowledge that practicing thinking presupposes ceasing breathing?

Philosophy is *thanato-praxis*. Philosophy is the 'I' dying the death of the 'we'.

For the philosopher the power of fundamental ideas to attribute significance to singularities and to determine significant orientations to collectives has something to do with the, often, barely perceptible demands of an era that whispers its secret. Ideas are announced first in and to the philosopher at a moment when no one can hear them. It is this 'no one' that possesses the philosopher. The philosopher is thus transformed into the bearer of a vision yet to come. In his singularity the philosopher's body is the empty house and his thinking/vision the silence of the glorious gatherings of the future. Or rather, his thinking is the vision of the vision, the exposure of the visionary in the defeated vision. Significance thus precedes correctness or incorrectness as a place of dwelling within which we can think questionably precisely because our being as thinkers has been saturated by answers, the answers these fundamental ideas themselves are. The primary challenge is, not to ask the question (for example, 'what is the meaning of being?'), but to withstand the intensity of the answer. Genuine questions always presuppose world-shaping answers. The anxiety of questioning presupposes the danger of an unlimited receiving. But receiving and the receiving of receiving are related to primordial states of the gathering and of ourselves as gathered and as gatherers. The fate of the philosopher is always determined by the kind of gathering that calls upon him to present himself as the gatherer, the bearer of the very idea, or vision, of the gathering. It is such visionary situatedness that reveals the gathering as philosophical. Philosophy arises in a philosophical world. Thus the challenge of the philosopher isn't simply to be the philosopher of the era but also to let the era emerge thinkingly as the era of the philosopher. Such thinking, though, unavoidably releases the thinker as the guardian of a world. He is the 'I' that, in the insignificance of its singularity, is called upon to utter 'we'. Or rather the 'I' comes across itself as this 'called upon'. Plato was the first guardian. Plato sought the eternity of the idea in a time determined by colliding worlds. He became the guardian of a world departing from the stage of history.

PARADOXES

1

Our era is the era of the time of time, the time of own-ability and the time of ownership. This is the time that is empty of eternity. The era to come will be the timeless in time.

2

In the present there is only future (longing) and therefore no present as presencing. In the future there will only be the present as fulfilled and fulfilling presencing and therefore no future.

3

Our era is that of the dispersion of mortals and that of the mortality of dispersion. The era to come will be that of the gathering of immortals and also that of the immortal gathering.

4

Today we are absent in our presence, pure creators with nothing to create. Tomorrow we'll be present in our absence, erotic receivers of absolute goodness and pure creators of the 'everything'.

Those who are absent in their presence emerge in the world as private property owners, cosmic gatherers of the indifference of Nature. (It is the act of owning in this fundamental sense that is presupposed by mathematics and by scientific knowing.) At the same time, they descent into the underworld of singularities populated neither by God nor by the gathering. The glory of God belongs to the past, and the glorious gatherings belong to the future. Thus singularity is emptied out and becomes the guardian of a secret, the insignificance of its own self-significance. Today, we are absolutely futural beings, unlimitedly saturated by the longing of the gathered who never was, and the gatherer who never became. The 'never was' and the 'never became' is our a-priori, our past who was never present, the past that by-passes the present, and under certain conditions points to the future. Under certain conditions the poet and the philosopher become the paradigmatic expression of such pointing to the future without future, the bearers of a visionary past, of a visionary state of death that never encountered life. It is the poet, and the philosopher, who are prepared to die the death of the gathering in us. The poet's singularity infinitely contracts and becomes the graveyard of those who never lived. The philosopher's singularity infinitely expands and becomes the visionary place of welcoming those who come from the future. In descending the poet utters the world 'love' or 'we'. In ascending, the philosopher in the poet also utters the same words. 'We' is the last word of poetry and the first word of philosophy. It is the word in the uttering of which the gathering gathers as a project to be realized.

The first philosopher is Plato. Not Socrates but Plato is the philosopher who dies the death of the gathering by retreating in its retreat.

'Hegel' is the retrieving of 'Plato'.

In Plato we have the vision of the gathering that, as vision, belongs to the past. It is the past as visionary. It is the vision of the very idea of the gathering that history leaves behind. In Hegel we have the vision of the gathering to come, the vision of erotic or communal singularities. Between them we have the unfolding of the historical into history as the field of dispersion of property owners, 'empty selves'. The field of dispersion is the field of the perpetual present that is released from the future and in turn releases the future.

The Greek gathering is the sculpting of the indifferent in the indifferent. The Greek gathering stays on the surface, on the skin of its collective body pointing towards the indifferent. It is the place from which the perfection of space is 'watched' and matter is experienced as being potentially the infinite bearer of form. The Greeks are true empiricists because they experience the aloneness of the gathering by becoming aware of the encompassing perfection of a Logos that is absolutely indifferent to us.

In the Greek gathering everybody is as gathered in a primordial sense. Everyone is in a pure state of manifestation without the innerness of manifesting. The gathering doesn't release individualities in order to make itself a project of regathering through them. The substantive bond of the collective fully claims individuals not by releasing them but by keeping them as gathered. In order to 'experience' its 'glowing' in the cosmic abyss, the Greek gathering imagines gods looking down at it.

How does the gathering 'escape' its Greek formulation? As gathered in the observing gathering the subject re-situates itself by detaching itself from substantive particulars of every kind. Nothing specific in the world can hold the subject 'out there'. Being in the world must be the subject's own achievement. But also by detaching itself from its detachment the subject lands in itself as singular, that is as pure willing. How does the subject 'move' back to the world? By dwelling in its singularity, by being the only agent that claims the subject, the will creates and receives itself by drawing the world in to the field of its awareness as the absolutely non-claiming: the subject has the vision of nothing claiming it. The indifferent, the perfection of externality of the Greek experience, is reintroduced, not as something observed, but as where the subject dwells. Indifference is the mode of being of the world, and the subject posits itself as its bearer. Therefore the subject infinitely saturates the indifferent by being infinitely saturated by it. The indifferent here is nature, or the natural in nature, and the subject reintroduces itself in the world precisely because it is the bearer of the world's mode of being. Now the subject deals with particulars not through their substantive content. Content becomes accessible once the object has been modified in terms that acknowledge externality as its mode of being. Such acknowledgement is ownership of 'things'. The subject's emerging in the world as owner in this radical sense is necessarily all-encompassing precisely because indifference and externality are all-encompassing delete. Dispersion is the state of being because encountering each other through owned 'things' creates an infinite distance between us. In so far as the subject dwells in its singularity through the vision of externality, it has access to universal space and time as forms of externality. This opens up the realm of the own-able. In so far as it owns, the subject finds itself in the relative time of exchange since it appears by attaching itself to a thing and withdraws by a like detaching. Here we have the time of time. As dispersed the self empties itself from being as gathered. But now, because of the democratic character of dispersion, it must also detach itself from the being of the gatherer. But as the gatherer never to be, the self comes from the future by denying the latter. In other words, it empties itself out of the possibility of being released by the global substantive gathering in order to say 'we'. But as released from the future in this negative sense, the gathering negates the kind of unboundedness that authentically belongs to the gathering as such, to the gathering that unconditionally receives itself without leaning on nature in any way. So in this negative manner the future 'invades' the global spaces of dispersion. The future is kept out through the intensification of exchange. At the same time being released from the future, the field of dispersed selves releases the future. The future is both drawn back in an act of implosion and is activated in an act of explosion. But to activate the future in these terms is to create the vision of the creation of significance out of insignificant singularities.

The ontology of liberalism gives rise to fascism: 'Being-Heidegger is one of my possibilities'. This realization, whose acceptance demands courage and alertness, is the reason why one must engage with this controversial thinker. The way to resist and move beyond Heidegger is to go through him. This is because the darkness of the gathering of the age is always *our* darkness, claiming us in a radical and uncompromising sense. To put it in terms reminiscent of Heraclitus, the fate of the thinker as the gathered-gatherer is the gathering itself since this fate is shaped, in an ultimate and unsurpassable way, by the possibilities of gathering already embedded in the historical gathering of the age. It is this that those who defend or criticize Heidegger forget. And it is precisely this axiomatic orientation that is ever present as the ever present throughout history that one should try not to forget. Heidegger is the thinker of Being because he is the philosopher of the gathering, and not the reverse. Of course this is also true for engaging with any other thinker who genuinely belongs to the gathering and in his thought articulates the very meaning of belonging. From this perspective, to be a thinker means to realize oneself as one of these possibilities in the paradigmatic and exemplary manner that philosophy demands. At the same time, it means to oppose the others as compromising the scope of the gathering, always terrified and perplexed by the proximity and the danger of the encounter. The primordial state of being as-gathered and as-gatherer in a more or less encompassing gathering doesn't allow the cultivation of neutral spaces for thinking, the beloved spaces of liberal minded thinkers. It imperatively seeks the commitment of the one who gathers as-gathered. In other words, the thinker encounters himself through the differentiation gathered-gatherer and is called upon by the situatedness of the differentiation itself to enact it by thinking, that is, by gathering concepts. The thinking of the gathering, the only possible subject matter for thinking, can be performed as the gathering of thinking itself. And in order for the thinker to be the gatherer of concepts he would have both to create and to receive them, to function in time in order to encounter eternity. Isn't this the true meaning of the encounter of the gathering with itself, namely, to receive as eternal what you, yourself, have created? And doesn't philosophy try to articulate the principle of this encounter? 'Being-Heidegger' then, is one of my possibilities because it is one of our possibilities. The other is that of 'being-Hegel'. Both belong to modernity as modernity's only genuine possibilities of being as-gathered and as-gatherer. But both also spring form the plane of history as reformulations of what the Plato of *The Republic* turned into the thinker's mission and the aim of thinking. Plato was the first—and in a sense also the last since those of us who come after him can only repeat the Plato-possibility by intensifying its scope in the context of the historical gathering that has intensified itself to the maximum—to understand and practice the axiomatic idea that philosophy arises in a philosophical world. And a philosophical world is always not one of enlightenment and promise, but one of darkness and death. This is the world of the human gathering in a state of schism, that between the impotent knowing of philosophy and the dispersed being of politics. It is in this schism and as this schism that the gathering sustains itself as the infinite source of intensity that enables it, not only to gather divinities and the whole of nature, but, ultimately, to gather its own self. The philosopher's head, a head that has lost its body, emerges by retreating in the spaces where the defeat of the gathering is first announced to be impossible precisely because the gathering has been defeated. It is only by defeating itself that the gathering proves to itself that it is undefeatable. And the first to announce this is the philosopher. Philosophical thinking is the shape the fumes of the dark vision of justice take rising out of the dismembered body of the *polis*. The challenge is thus set, not so much to question as to withstand and survive in the realization that the reconciliation the philosopher seeks with humanity is the reconciliation humanity itself seeks with itself. And it is this challenge that takes the thinker beyond the calm state required for the asking of the impossible question, 'why is there something rather than nothing', to a state of panic that gives rise to the impossible asking of the question, 'why is there nothing rather than something?'. Philosophy presupposes the panicking of disorientation, the instant scepticism of a detachment that belongs to the love of the most intense attachment, that towards the *polis*. Philosophy then is either the asceticism of a conceptually disciplined madness activated out of the experience of the death of the gathering's erotic body, or it is nothing at all.

There are three Heideggers: The Heidegger of *Being and Time* who is as-gathered; the Heidegger of the nineteen-thirties who is the gatherer with a gathering; and the later Heidegger who is the gatherer without a gathering.

The mystery of the dead God doesn't compare in intensity with the mystery of the dead gathering.

Why does the scientific knowledge of nature rely on mathematics? Because knowing presupposes owning; it presupposes accessibility to nature's mode of being, and mathematics is the thinking of owning.

The primary question is, not 'what is mathematics' but 'who is the mathematician'?

The challenge isn't to understand the meaning of creating something out of nothing, but of creating something out of something.

The ego is porous like a sieve. It is history that passes through it.

Pure difference is an orphan.

The field of the defeat of language is the erotic body loved by the gathering, the purely inner.

The indeterminate gathering retreats from the land of history and takes the position of the ocean.

The scandal of Heidegger studies is their inability to retrieve *Being and Time* through the question of being, just as the scandal of Hegel studies is the failure to reflect on the *Philosophy of Right* through the logical categories.

Heidegger's philosophy is that of the era. But the era he reveals isn't that of philosophy.

According to Castoriadis, the 'Greco-Western creation of Logos and Reason' arises with the question: 'What are we to think?' When thinking appears, it seeks its proper subject matter. But, the implication here is that genuine thinking always appears as for the first time and so encounters itself by repeating the same fundamental question in the context of the given historical moment. From this perspective, the challenge the ancient philosophers faced is still very much with us today. The proper question for thinking, in the primordial state of encountering itself and attempting to identify its mission and place in the era of modernity, is not the question of the meaning of being (Heidegger), or the doubting of an insecure subjectivity overwhelmed by the instability and relativism of meanings (Descartes), not even the question of the conditions of the possibility of knowledge (Kant). The more primordial question is 'What are we to think?' This question springs from and points to both a state of collective being shaped by the possibility of exercising radical thinking and the relation of the thinker and thinking to the human gathering and its condition. In a simple and direct manner, the asking of the question achieves a kind of scepticism towards any sort of given in so far as it focuses attention on the autonomous orientation that determines the very character of thinking. By asking the question the questioner is taken beyond the Cartesian tradition of subject-centred, piecemeal doubting to thinking as the agent that, in seeking its proper subject matter, negates any kind of pre-determined grounding. Paradoxically though, because of the 'intensity' involved in this question and the associated questioning, an intensity powerful enough to make explicit the field of and the initial task of thinking, one gets the sense that the 'what' that the question reveals doesn't itself exhaust the question of thinking. The formulation of this fundamental question, and precisely because it is fundamental, is rather inadequate. Perhaps an answer to the question 'what are we to think?' can be given as follows: 'We are to think what matters'. But such a response, even if formally correct, is incomplete. Where would thinking get its call, so to speak, to think what matters if not from what matters itself? In the absence of such a call, thinking would be at a loss because the thinker would have to think before thinking in seeking the subject matter for thinking. In order for thinking to think what matters, thinking itself must matter by somehow *belonging* to what matters. If thinking what matters, presupposes a relating to and an acknowledgement of a 'where', the 'what' question must be supplemented with the 'where' question: 'what are we to think and where are we to be situated in order to think it?' However, even this expanded version of the question is still not broad enough. It seems that it must be further supplemented given philosophy's imperative emphasis on the social-historical situatedness of the thinker: 'what are we to think, where and when are we to think it?' But if the 'what', the 'where', and the 'when' are not natural givens for the thinking, neither is thinking's mode of activity, its 'how'. So the 'what', 'where', 'when', and 'how' form four dimensions of the question characterizing the activation of genuine thinking. Now if we treat this multidimensional question as the question of thinking itself—as the philosophical question that opens the field of radical reflection—we might give an answer in the following form. The challenge for thinking is to think what matters in a manner that matters at a place and time that matter. But if we are to think what matters in a manner that matters then our thinking must somehow belong to what is to be thought and be activated by it and in it as the thinking that itself matters. In a certain sense, thinking would be nothing less than the intensification, deepening, or expansion of this very belonging articulated by the 'what-where-when-how' of thinking. From this suggestion though, and rather unexpectedly, something significant follows: the question of the 'what-where-when-how' presupposes the response to another perhaps more foundational question: 'ought we to think at all?' If this is indeed the case, then it seems that the 'what-where-when-how' question can be asked only after the 'ought' question receives an affirmative answer. The 'ought' question is necessarily prior because, unlike the 'what-where-when-how' question, it has the capacity to directly address the singular being of the thinker himself and his relation to what matters, as the fundamental pre-condition for the activation of thinking and its question(s) as states of being concerned with what matters in a manner that matters. In other words, thinking and its question(s) presuppose the situatedness and emergence of the thinker in what matters, or more precisely, they presuppose the transformation of one into a thinker, that is, into one who matters, precisely because this is what it would mean for one to 'dwell' in what matters. But now something else equally unexpected appears. Being informed, or 'claimed', by what matters as a thinker makes it impossible for the thinker to respond negatively to the 'ought' question. This is the same as saying that the 'ought' question has one and only one possible answer. In order for one to actually ask it the thinker must take the perspective of a single and affirmative answer, which the thinker himself, in his own being, must be qua being claimed as thinker by what matters. In being claimed as a thinker by what matters, one is posited as the significant receiver of a universal imperative to think; and consequently, as already and always being the bearer of thinking what matters in the very 'place' and 'time' of being claimed. Before thinking asks the question of its proper subject matter that which matters has claimed the thinker and thinking as significant. But then it is such claiming that not only makes the thinker and thinking significant, it also provides thinking with its subject matter, as well as the place and time of its happening. It is obvious that if thinking is to start at all, it must be challenged not by fundamental questions but by radical answers. From this perspective, it follows that questions come after the answer as a way of simply reminding us that the real challenge for the thinker comes from the answer to be thinkingly articulated. But, equally, it is the nature of the claiming that also determines the 'how' of thinking. Thinking unfolds by refolding and 'falling' back into the 'where' of the thinker's situatedness in a perpetual re-capturing of the command to think. So the 'answer' to the 'ought' question is the thinker himself, and he is the answer in his capacity as that which already belongs to what matters. He is a thinker before thinking. The meaning of 'belonging' is of course the crucial issue here.

History is the serial killing of the descending philosopher by the city.

Philosophers talk, poets face.

The gathering is oceanic.

It is only as (di)vision that the gathering reaches its depth, the under-world of its world.

Speculative philosophy is an activity that takes place under extreme circumstances. Here however the extreme is not understood as a boundary that points to a beyond. The extreme is the meeting place of the same, simplicity encountering itself; it is the same at the point where it unfolds and refolds in its unfolding.

Owning is the impurity at the core of personhood.

Metaphysics was the manifesto of the rebel.

My self is revealed in its departure form the gathering, which is not a departure at all. This is the infinite contradiction, which in speculative philosophy emerges not as the source of destruction but as the spring of spiritual being. Possibly then at the crossroads of its schism the gathering emerges in all the glory of its creative power since it shows itself able to create love from the depths of its own death by creating significance out of utter contingency. The power of such glory cannot be appreciated even at the stage where spirit moves beyond history to the completion of its circle. The desire that time is, is infinitely more intense and revealing than its satisfaction. The intensity of the desire is infinite-absolute otherness. Hegel is the philosopher of the intensity of desire. The point of philosophy isn't to move beyond desiring to a state of some completion. The point here is the criterion of 'satisfaction', which is a satisfaction-less satisfaction.

That something is beyond time means that time is incorporated in it. It preserves itself in time by moving deeper into what it already is. It is a coming back, a recapturing of itself, a moving deeper, of becoming quietly and silently more intensive that time is manifested. Time here is the infinity of becoming what has already become. Time is overflowing.

Between us and Hegel nothing has happened. In the non-event of philosophical time Hegel, that is, we, remains the great unknown.

Poetry becomes the despair of simplicity. Philosophy turns this despair into vision.

Simplicity permits a non-perspectival awareness. The simplicity of death liberates us from the myth of perspective.

The simplicity of the simple is indiscernible difference, 'grey on grey'.

The extreme is non-referential and thus it is immune to any kind of external limit. Once in the extreme, the philosopher realizes the futility of hoping and the majesty of the freedom of non-being. It is then that he becomes the bearer of the idea of pulsating by himself pulsating between death and love. This is Hegel's negative moment; the internal dividing of what eternally sustains itself even when it reaches itself as its own extreme. 'Infinite pain' then is not just a possibility; it is spirit's moment of ultimate transparency since self-knowledge is constantly mediated by the otherness of self-loss(being), the most radical form of self-reference.

The moment it detects its boundaries being jumps outside itself.

The emptying out of the gathering creates unbearable inwardness. Here presence and absence come together. One belongs to the other. As absence presence becomes infinitely heavy. We can collapse under the weight of our own presence. Philosophy accepts the collapse, and even celebrates it.

The task after Hegel is to speak simply.

Explosion is repeating.

To take responsibility for our birth; this is the challenge. Away from such an act the world is indifferent to us.

Philosophy always starts from one of two fundamental experiences: either we are relevant to the world or we are irrelevant.

Change has the form of exchange.

Pure difference is exchange.

Only others can celebrate my birth, and only others can mourn my death. The other totally claims me.

As returning, the 'I' returns as 'We'.

In the world to come philosophy will be a thing of the past. The participants of this world will discover that the moment of pure conceptualization (of the majestic and impotent innerness) has already happened and that their world has already conceptually happened in the happening of this moment. They will be in a position to understand themselves through their past by reading the speculative story of world Spirit that the philosophers have already prepared. On this reading, philosophers like Hegel are the Homers of the people of the future who will in turn be the genuine readers of philosophy.

Capitalism's authority is derived from the future.

Language is always potentiality, that of love.

Why does one feel the need to open one's soul to a perfect stranger?

At the moment of wonder the Greek philosopher is like an atom expanding once the journey of knowledge begins. The aim is to map the entire scene and then dwell in this mapping.

THE COMMAND

1

If for the gathering the command, 'be as a world', is not imposed by God but is part of the fabric of the gathering itself then the gathering needs to posit not only itself as the command but also itself as the agent who receives it. As both the command and its receiving the gathering is the simple out of which the difference between the command and its reception is posited.

2

In manifesting itself as the manifestation to become, the gathering creates a disturbance (restlessness) out of the state of tranquillity. Its possibility is thus also its actuality and it realizes this possibility through the creation out of itself of the difference between the command and its reception.

3

As commanding the ethical gathering is the whole to be-come. The gathering is coming and becoming because it has already come and become. The command is infinite; it does not fail to be received and to be obeyed. As the received command it fully manifests itself. It is the whole and the power to realize itself. The agent receiving the universal gathering as a command receives it as what must become. In this receiving the gathering is as received and also as not receiving itself. The universal gathering that is received, received that is by its other, is the 'not yet'. Here time is released in the fulfilment of time. That which is completely in time, the absolutely insignificant, is released by the absolute significance of the timeless. A differentiation of form and content is thus activated. In their togetherness, the form of receiving the universal gathering and the universal's content as received manifest the negation of the universal, the not yet. As received and in being received by its insignificant other, the universal commands the other to transcend itself and become the bearer of significance in order for the universal gathering to be realized. The agency that functions both as the other of the universal gathering and as the recipient of the universal command, is the finitude of the particular ego. This is the miracle of the speculative. The gathering is the magical power of transforming the insignificant ego into the significant missionary as the gatherer of the universal gathering. As the agent receiving the command of the universal gathering, the particular acts as the *topos* of the not yet of the universal. This means that the command commands in and through the particular's receiving. But the particular is in a position to perform the role of receiving the universal when it provides the gathering with its pure notion without providing the universal's being. It follows that, as the bearer of the notion of the universal, the being of the particular is also the negation of the universal—the absolute singularity of the particular. This is the particular that thinks; it is finite mind. In this capacity the particular does not lose itself in its particularity in the process of receiving the command. It is that which thinks or receives the universal of the whole as the universal to become and thus receives itself as the agent of enacting the whole. The particular then is as thinking. In being as thinking the particular experiences the differentiation of being and thinking as a differentiation that must be overcome.

4

The gathering is the immediately realized whole that is also posited as realizable. Through such positing it recaptures itself as realized, albeit only immediately. Once fully realized through the execution of what the command commands, the gathering overcomes the contradiction of simplicity and difference, or substance and subject, without however forgetting their difference. It incorporates itself as realizable by recollecting the command and its receiving. It thus perpetually renews itself as the already realized gathering—that is, as the result of the gathering's circular movement that repeatedly retrieves its beginning and realizes its end. Here what is realized cannot fail also to be as both realizing and realizable. But this presupposes the primordially realized which is thus unrealizable, that is, unthinkable. This is the supreme moment of togetherness (Paul Celan) of those who are together.

5

Both states of the gathering—its forward movement, through which it posits itself as realizable and ultimately as realized, and its backward movement of recollection from its state of completion—rely upon the mediating power of the moment of the command and its reception. In both of its forms such a state manifests the 'not' at the centre of the gathering. This state is the gathering's power to mediate between its immediate and its mediated states of being the whole. As this power of mediation the absolute is the mutual informing of the infinity of its command with the finitude of its reception.

6

Hegel observes that 'absolute Spirit [...] opposes to itself another spirit, the finite, the principle of which is to know absolute spirit, in order that absolute spirit may become existent for it'. The absolute spirit is what withstands the opposition between the infinite command and its finite reception. As being received by the finite, the infinite does not crush the finite. So too, as receiving the infinite, the finite does not distort the infinite. Consequently, as the creator of its own opposition, the gathering already contains in itself that which, when released, posits both its infinite command and finite spirits as the agents of receiving and activating the command through their receiving. It follows that in the gathering's state of being immediately what it must become, finite spirits are already incorporated in some form of gathering—the immediate communal being—that affirms that the gathering is immediately the whole. It is out of this gathering that the gathering posits the command together with finite spirits as the command's recipients. In doing so the gathering posits finite spirits as beings with the appropriate form of agency for receiving its command. Indeed, by positing individualized unities, the gathering posits a form that involves dispersal and so negates the immediate universal communal unity of the agents in question.

7

The finite receives, and its finitude is to be as receiving. If the principle of the finite is to receive the command 'Know Thyself' and if the being of the finite is its receiving the command (and thus activating the commanding), then the finite manifests the very principle of finitude in the specificity of its receiving being. At the same time it also renders explicit the very meaning of the command since the command can be received only by the agent capable of providing its meaning. If the command commands me to know myself and if 'know' involves no specification, then I can only know myself as receiver of the command to know that I am already positioned to receive in so far as I provide the very meaning of knowing. So the command manifests as command in the field opened up by the activation of its meaning through the agency of the finite.

8

If, as the agent of receiving the command through its specificity, the specific finite spirit provides the meaning of the command and the principle of finite spirit, finite spirit must also be the embracing of all finite spirits.

This is because in enabling the command to command through its receiving and in thereby receiving the received—the gathering that in already being what it must become has already gathered the finite spirits in itself—the gathered finite spirits must themselves dwell in the single finite spirit as the receiver of the command. This landing of the infinite in the finite makes it possible for the finite unconditionally to embrace every particular spirit as already gathered by the gathering and hence as what must be gathered. That is, it makes it possible for the finite to embrace communal being. Due to its powerless power to receive the command the singularity of the finite spirit is also an infinite expansion that is the place of dwelling or the gathering of the already gathered finite spirits in their capacity as the gathered to become. This state manifests the power to gather out of which what is commanded is to be realized. In other words, what receives the command is what the gathering already is and must become, namely immediate communal being gathered in the singularity of the 'I'. That it must become is manifested in that its bearer is the singular mind whose mode of being is one of dispersal. Here the absolute is the 'I' that is in a position to say 'we'. The command commands finite spirits to gather since, as already being what it must become, absolute spirit immediately affirms itself by incorporating finite spirits as gathered into its field of self affirming.

9

To posit finite spirit as the receiver of the command is simultaneously to manifest what the gathering is and that it must become what it is. The gathering is affirmed, as both, in being received as the command by the gathered finite spirit. Finite spirit must itself simultaneously dwell in both moments: it must dwell in the gathering of finite spirits that the gathering already incorporates and yet in receiving the gathering as command, finite spirit manifests the not yet of the gathering. In this second role as receiver finite spirit dwells in the world of finite spirits that must be gathered and, as the not yet gathered, remain in a state of dispersal. Therefore as command the gathering commands finite spirits to re-gather or to become what they already are. In so commanding the infinite is itself the power that gathers or the gathering itself.

10

The gathering is always already itself or the whole. But it also must become the whole that it is. This task is made explicit in the self-positing of the gathering as a project to be realized. Here the gathering is realized without however laying to rest the power of realizing.

11

The gathering is the immediate gathered-gathering that ultimately formulates itself as the gathering-gathered—the gathered that involves the appropriate knowing as gathering—through the reflective moment of self-dispersal.

12

The gathering is absolute irrespective of its particular mode of being because it always performs the impossible.

The gathering is immediate yet without sinking into or evaporating in its immediacy and so without moving beyond its immediacy in whatever form. In its state of immediacy the challenge for the gathering is to not lose its absoluteness in the light of its state of immediacy. The immediate absolute must remain an absolute immediacy, an affirming immediacy. Here immediacy is the mode of being that determines mediation or, in other words, 'differencelessness' is the mode of being of the gathering that determines difference.

13

Being an affirming immediacy the gathering does not go beyond itself into the externality of otherness in order to affirm itself in a mediating way through some return to itself from the state of otherness or self-loss. Even though this is the ultimate aim of the gathering such a move nevertheless presupposes the immanent affirmation of what must be superseded as well as the activation of the superseding process through such affirmation rather than despite it. Precisely because the gathering does not lose itself in its state of immediacy, it is also the power to move beyond to its other moments of self-realization. The reverse is also the case. Because it is the power of moving beyond, it can also affirm itself in its immediacy. Moreover, the gathering is the power to move beyond in so far as it has already moved beyond. The task is for this movement to be perpetually recollected from within the moments of its development.

14

In order to be both immediate and affirming the gathering must go deeper into what already is the case for it and hence to stay with what it already is. So the reality of the gathering calls not for a transition but for unlimited intensification of its already realized affirmation. We should understand the immediate as incorporating mediation within itself, albeit without going beyond its own immediacy. The immediate is a return-without-going-beyond. In the mode of being of immediacy the ethical gathering moves with infinite speed in the infinite depth of its immobility.

15

Affirmation involves difference, difference involves otherness and otherness involves mediation. In order for immediate affirmation to be affirming it therefore needs an other, albeit one in whom the gathering does not lose itself in order to return to itself in a triumphant gesture of accomplishment. It requires of otherness not that it should enable immediacy to pass through it to something else but that it may stay where it already is and thereby traverse the infinity of its remaining where it always already is. This is the realization already involved in what is already realized as intensification or deepening. If the immediate is affirming in so far as it is the infinite power of affirming itself in its other, then moving deeper into itself means moving towards its other as itself or itself as its other. How can the immediate be both itself and its other in a way that manifests its power to locate in its other only itself?

16

After history the gathering is a return without self-loss. Returning means infinitely intensifying what is already the case or as Hegel says 'boundless blessedness'. What is the other of the universal gathering that the universal is, yet without losing itself? It is the already permeated and embraced particular ego that the universal permeates and embraces. Thanks to the immediacy that belongs to the other itself the gathering's erotic equality with itself retains its immediacy in the particular and thereby affirms this immediacy in and as such retaining. The other of the universal neither expresses the loss of the immediate universal nor offers it a place of dwelling by providing the universal with its notion. The other neither 'expels' the immediate absolute nor 'receives' it. In other words the particular is non-thinking, immediate singularity. It is the immediate and infinite embraced that the universal immediately and infinitely embraces. In embracing it the universal 'finds' in its other the other as always already embraced by the universal. The universal is the power of love of its other who is already 'living' in love, a power that its other drives to intensification.

17

With the immediacy's determination of the mediation the embracing is only embracing and, correspondingly, the embraced is only embraced. Accordingly, the embraced particular excludes embracing and does not itself embrace the universal gathering in order thereby to transform the embracing into the embraced. What would it mean for the embraced also to embrace the universal? It would offer the very idea of the universality of the gathering and in this way function as the *topos* of the universal. Instead, thinking is excluded here. The universal is thought, but immediately so, since it is not received by the embraced as the agent who thinks or embraces the universal. It follows that the embraced particular does not manifest any form of agency. Moreover, in not reflectively relating to itself it does not make possible its own thematization of its embraced being. This is the essence of its 'blindness'. Being unable to receive thought by thinking it, the embraced being manifests a form of awareness that is blind to thought itself or indeed anything beyond itself. It is an unthinking thought that thought occupies immediately. The embraced being is thus always already open to the universal that in turn, finding itself in the embraced being, takes the particular beyond itself towards the universal. It is in this movement of the universal—of taking beyond as this taking beyond—that the particular is determined as lacking agency.

18

The universal gathering is beyond the particular gathered because it is beyond any particular. In fact, it marks the beyond in a dual sense: it is beyond its embracing of the particular not only because it can also ceaselessly embrace another particular and another but also because the universal is the world of embracing. After all, the particular is embraced in the world of embracing. This is another way of saying that the universal is the power of gathering the particulars which particulars always already manifest the being of being gathered. It is in the particular as gathered that the universal finds itself. At the same time as the other of the universal in which the universal returns to itself the gathered particular is an individual, that is, it has integrity.

19

The universal gathering's embracing gathers the particulars as already gathered by the universal power of the gathering bond. Here, the particular does not recognize itself as gathered and so does not involve itself in acts of gathering. The particular is always already gathered; its being is gathered being. Its being is completely determined by the universality of the always already realized gathering. So the universal is both infinitely (non)divided and the infinite embracing of such (non)division. It is the 'differencelessness' that incorporates difference. Here we have intrinsically communal being as a world, yet without communality understood as the reflective element of the notion that makes manifestation possible. Here the moment of universality is the life of communal being without the happening of the reflective appropriation of such being. Communal being is thus without its happening. Yet this non-happening is infinitely affirmative. The philosophical task then is to show how the gathering releases its manifestation through the moments of its self-releasing in and through which the gathering recollects itself. Each moment thus becomes a form of the gathering as a whole and the power that releases the other forms. This is why the act of superseding one moment through the release of a second, 'higher', moment also activates the release of the first and a return of the second to the first. It also explains why even in its fully realized state the gathering releases its previous moments in a perpetual movement of recollection as perpetual recreation. In exploding so to speak from its state of immediacy to its state of realized manifestation the gathering also implodes into the primordial state of immediacy in order to reactivate itself through the recollection of the primordial activation. Plato was the first to intuit the pulse of the gathering.

20

The universal gathering is as the world of embracing. The gathering is always a world.

21

In the mode of being of immediacy the gathering is immediately complete and thus infinite. So it must release itself from the simplicity of its completeness into a state of incompleteness or finitude. Being immediate it must release itself as immediate that is as the immediate that recognizes that its immediacy is already mediated by its power to be, a power that is itself mediated by the fact that it can be. Consequently the gathering releases itself as a project to be realized, a project that locates its justification and draws its inspiration from its very completeness. It is thus a project but not in time.

22

In the mode of being of immediate completeness the universal gathering finds itself in the particular but it does not recognize itself in it as the power to be; it simply is. In a sense such an encounter is also a loss since locating itself in the immediate is itself an immediate locating that excludes the thinking that is associated with the notion of the gathering. Still, because it incorporates otherness, the immediate is infinitely affirming and thus nevertheless powerful enough not only to affirm itself in its immediacy but also to affirm itself as the immediate that is able to be.

23

In so far as the gathering is a project because it is complete the moment of otherness manifests its affirmative power as absolute negation. With the release of the gathering's immediacy through the positing of otherness—the release that renders explicit the gathering's power of realization —the gathering is released as the not yet and hence as the absolutely not.

24

Because the gathering is itself 'not', it withdraws in and as this not. This is the moment of finitude, the moment that, in exhibiting its power to be the absolute, is not yet. But this is also affirmation, the element of recognition in negation that renders the negation absolute since it posits the aim of affirming that the affirmed is not yet the affirming affirmed. It is as this not that the gathering relates itself to itself. In other words its negativity is absolute because it is also a self-relation.

25

How exactly does the gathering manifest itself in the mode of being of particularity simultaneously as absolute negativity and as self-recognition in the form of a project? The moment of particularity is also the infinite division of the immediacy or simplicity characterizing the moment of universality. As this division the moment of universality is retrieved as an aim to be realized and as a realizable aim. Its realizability has already been demonstrated both in the affirming of the whole that the moment of universality is and through this moment's power of negativity in releasing its immediate being. As such it has shown itself to be the realizable whole that formulates itself as the project that is in the process of realizing itself.

26

The moment of particularity is division, the dispersal of particulars and hence the positing of their singularity, something that the universal gathering has previously absorbed. Even so particularity is not a state of affairs that depends upon the external differentiation of particulars; it is instead the mode of being of the particulars. Particularity is thus the universal condition of particulars and hence the universal itself. So it is a way of gathering the particulars. However, in so far as gathering is also a dispersing, gathering as dispersing is the gathering as the aim to become what it is not yet. Transforming dispersal into the gathering-to-be is the absolute power of gathering. Here the universal gathering re-emerges as a task. The gathering that gathers those that have yet to be gathered—the dispersed ones—is a gathering yet to come. Accordingly the universal cannot yet embrace the particular as gathered but only as what must become gathered. In recognizing itself as an aim—in recognizing its not that dispersal manifests—the universal is transformed into a command. It transforms itself into a task by commanding the particular to be as gathered. Here the infinite blends with the finite. Whereas the command is infinite, its reception is finite. The infinite is precisely received as what must become and hence as what is not. But the universality of dispersing is also the retrieval of the immediate universal and therefore of the universal that has already gathered the particulars. So the universal commands the particular to gather as the immediately and hence already gathered.

27

The particular ego is the gathered-dispersed that manifests its power to gather by receiving the gathering as a command. It must recognize, or rather, it is the recognition of dispersal as its mode of being since the particular is already beyond the pure state of immediacy in which it dwells as immediately gathered and thereby manifests its singularity. In so far as this recognition is possible and necessary, in recognizing particularity as the mode of being of the particular the particular is also the recognition of the universal as a command. The particular must be the power of receiving the command without being crushed by this reception. This involves the particular in thinking since it can only receive the universal as a command and thereby activate the latter's commanding by providing the notion of the universal—the notion of the gathering. So as thinking, the finite performs the impossible; it survives the reception of the infinite. This is the speculative miracle of finitude, the very idea of the finite. But the finite can only do this as gathered. From immediately being gathered the particular moves to the reflecting state of being as immediately gathered. It does this by turning its being into the receiving of the gathering as the command to gather or as the command for it to become what it already is, namely gathered and therefore to receive the command as gatherable. This is also none other than a retrieve of immediate communal being in its entirety—that is as universal—as receiving the command to become or as capable of being communally. Here the particular is the being of communal being, albeit in a thinking manner that provides the notion of the universal in order to receive the universal as command.

28

The particular receives the command by generating the mutual embracing of being and notion out of itself. It is this being/notion inter-relation that makes possible the universality of the gathering as command in terms of the thinking or receiving of thought. It is the command that commands the realization of the mutual embracing of being and notion. Here we have the explicit genesis of conceptuality, that is, the conceptual emergence of the absolute as manifestation, as the realizable that is also to be realized in the immobility of its unrealizability.

29

Two different forms of immediacy characterize the immediate whole in its respective connections with the universal as command and the particular as receiving the command. Even though it is this whole that both commands and receives the command, it nevertheless does so in a way that retains two forms of immediacy as separate and self-subsistent. One is the form of the particular as gathered—in the immediacy of its being the particular provides thinking as the notion of the universal and therefore as gatherable—and the other is the form of the universal as gathering—it is the power to bring about gathering.

30

Because the particular receives the universal gathering as command by providing the universal's notion and because the universal commands in this receiving of the particular the commanding of the command is manifested in the form of the individual. The realm of particularity or dispersing happens as a command in the particular that incorporates the universal as an individual and thus transforms itself into a totality. This is the logical articulation of the idea of the 'I' that is 'we'. This is perhaps the absolute speculative mystery, the mystery of absolute singularity that in receiving the command of the communal 'we' is transformed into the bearer of the 'we' that commands every single 'I'.

31

The totality is the indeterminate gathering whose indeterminacy manifests as the command to create form. Indeterminacy concerns the retrieval of the immediate whole as something that must become and this becoming must involve the creation of a structured whole. So the indeterminate is the activity of retrieving/positing; it retrieves the whole in order to render it an aim. Still, what is retrieved does the commanding and receiving. This latter is immediate being that must happen as what it is and can only happen in the *topos* of its notion. The question of the notion/ being inter-relation becomes explicit in the realm of the indeterminate gathering. The realm of the indeterminate gathering posits that which creates being and notion out of itself as self-manifesting, or the absoluteness of the absolute, and through this positing the absolute is itself also posited as an aim to be realized.

32

The command of the gathering is empty; it is purely a command without commanding something specific. Accordingly, the 'what' of the command that is received is the purity of thought in its complete indeterminacy. Moreover, it is received in so far as the particular ego offers it its notion, the notion of thought, which is none other than pure thinking. The command is thought and commands thinking that is activated as the notion of thinking, that is, as thinking that receives thought. In order for thinking to receive thought it cannot just be a thinking about thought; it must be a thinking thought and it is a thinking thought because what is thinking is the thinking particular, that is in itself universal. In this way thinking already incorporates being and being already incorporates thinking.

33

Each particular ego is the *topos* of the gathering. The gathering of egos is thus a gathering of infinite gatherings. As members of the indeterminate gathering, individuated individuals encounter each other as both commanding the other and receiving the command from the other. They greet each other with 'be as a world' or 'know thyself'. For this reason individual egos are exactly like one another—the other is like me in that he or she also receives and commands—and yet there is an infinite asymmetry in the inter-relation of individuals in so far one commands and the other receives.

34

The gathering never remains in the mode of being of an aim to be realized and it never limits itself to the mode of being of the realized that has forgotten its realizing. The realized gathering is the power of infinite construction and infinite deconstruction. It never allows its fully established world of gathering to transform itself into a lifeless given by cutting its ties with its very power to be created as a world. Its fullness relates to the fact that it is at once fully realized and also radically yet to be realized. Nevertheless it allows itself to be absorbed in the immediate element of its unity and does not permit the systematization of its difference to become systemic in a way that would empower this difference to destroy its immediate unity.

The command to be as a world that is linked to the creation of form out of the formless gathering is what commands those gathered to gather. Since it is the gathering that must gather itself, the formed gathering must be a gathering of gatherings. Each particular form of gathering must be a particular manifestation of the world of the gathering of gatherings. Not only must the particular forms be gathered as aspects of the universal gathering but also each particular form must realize the gathering of gatherings, that is, each particular form must realize the whole. Accordingly, we might expect the unity of the moments of particularity and universality, the moment of individuality to be a unity of three syllogisms whose form manifests the whole as the gathering of gatherings. In Hegel's system this logical inter-relation will manifest existentially as the moments of the constitution of the ethical state wherein 'each [of these moments] contains the other moments and has them effective in itself'. When we are informed by the ideas of gathering and dispersal we are in a position to appreciate how this existential manifestation of the syllogistic unity results from the gathering's 'fragrant rising up' out of the 'foaming ferment of its finitude'.

'Like you, I always feared that I would not have time for it all' (George Michelakakis).

Adieu

www.ingramcontent.com/pod-product-compliance
Lightning Source LLC
Chambersburg PA
CBHW030220170426
43194CB00007BA/809